A Practical Guide to S

SOCIAL GRACES

SUE ANN CORDELL

I want to hear from you. Please send your comments about this Bible study to Sue Ann Cordell at sueann@shineworthy.com. Thank you!

SHINEWORTHY LIFESTYLES
A Positive Approach to Life!
www.shineworthy.com | sueann@shineworthy.com

SOCIAL GRACES

A PRACTICAL GUIDE TO SURVIVING THE HOLIDAYS

ACKNOWLEDGEMENTS

This book is dedicated to the men and women who have been a part of my family traditions since I was a small child. You have inspired me and instilled the importance of tradition into the very core of my soul.

Thank you to my #1 encourager - my husband, Randy.

I am grateful for my editor, Kathy Zeigler, for her expertise.

Special thanks to Becky Bayne of Becky's Graphic Design. You are extremely talented, and I am blessed to have you on my team!

Thank you Lois McGhee (Mom) for your generosity, love, and precious holiday memories. You are truly an inspiration to me. Thanks for the memories!

Thank you to my children, Hether and her husband Rustin, Bobby and his wife Michelle and my grandchildren, Randi, Rowan, Riley, and Claire. You bring such joy and happiness to our home during the holidays, and throughout the year!

Thank you God for the gift of your Son!

TABLE OF CONTENTS

SOCIAL GRACES

INTRODUCTION

The holiday season is just around the corner, and I look forward to spending the next six weeks offering you practical guidelines for surviving the hustle and bustle of the holidays. We will look at new patterns of doing things, new thought habits, and fun and exciting ways to decorate, bake, and entertain throughout the season.

I have written these lessons in a way that relates to struggles and challenges that women face in their everyday life. I combine biblical teachings, humor, and holiday ideas in hopes of making this your best holiday season yet.

I encourage you to take time each day to complete the assigned lesson and to make every effort to attend the group sessions once a week. There is no better way to enjoy the holidays than the ways God has planned for you. He created you to experience contentment, joy, and hope.

I pray that you will find strength for each day and a bright hope for tomorrow as you discover ways to survive the holidays.

Sue Ann Cordell

WEEK 1

ATTITUDE OF GRATITUDE

Enjoy the things of life while you can. If we are not careful, we will find ourselves taking things for granted and missing out on some of the blessings that God has planned for us. When I think about this, I am reminded of the lyrics to an old song that goes like this, "Don't it always seem to go that you don't know what you've got 'til it's gone? They paved Paradise and put up a parking lot."

In this first week of study, we will look at ways to shift our mindsets toward people and circumstances with an attitude of gratitude that is pleasing to God.

Anticipate all God wants to teach you this week! Ask Him to show you the things He wants you to see every day as you study His word. Be open to a fresh new approach to life!

DAY 1
Praise the
Lord!

DAY 2
Thank God for
Teachers!

DAY 3
A True Friend
Is a Rare Find

DAY 4
At Least I Have
a Job

DAY 5
The Value of a
Church Family

DAY 1
PRAISE THE LORD!

PRAISE THE LORD!

What does it mean to praise the Lord? For me, it means to show honor and respect to Him in all that I do. When I praise the Lord, I sing songs, I pray, and most importantly, I live my life with an attitude of gratitude. Every decision that I make reflects my attitude whether I like it or not. If I stay focused on praising the Lord with my attitude, I look at things through His eyes and not with selfish motives. As a child of the King, I have every reason in the world to praise the Lord and so do you!

PRAISE HIM IN SONG.

I love to sing and catch myself humming tunes throughout the day. You don't have to be an accomplished vocalist to praise the Lord in song. Even if you can't carry a tune at all, you can listen to praise and worship music that others have recorded and sing along. There are so many different genres of music out there these days, and you can find a style that suits you if you try.

I love all kinds of music. Sometimes I listen to majestic "high church" songs of praise. On other days I might listen to black gospel or Christian rock. Some days I long for the sounds of Southern gospel, traditional hymns, and country. My favorite way to praise the Lord in song is to sing from my heart with no outside help, just me singing praises to the Lord "acapella style." Some might say I'm singing "squackypella style," but I believe no matter how it may sound to those around us, it is truly music to God's ears because He knows it is coming from the heart!

A good way to start the day is by listening to praise music. In the mornings as your family members come into the kitchen for their breakfast, whether it be a cup of coffee, cereal, pop tart, or a full meal, why not have praise music playing in the background? I have been doing this since my children were small. There have been many mornings when a song of praise to the Lord has changed my attitude before walking out the door, and the same has been true for my family.

When driving to work or carpooling your children to school, play praise music. It will start your day in the right frame of mind and help you have an attitude of gratitude that otherwise might have been overlooked.

PRAISE HIM IN PRAYER.

Everything that is good comes from God. Take time each day to acknowledge your gratitude through prayer. Begin your prayers with thanksgiving for all the good things He has done for you. He is our helper and provides hope. He is the one who made heaven and earth, the sea, and everything in them. He formed you in your mother's womb. He keeps every promise forever. He provides all of our needs. He cares about everything that happens to us. He takes care of orphans and widows.

Even on the days when you feel down or trauma strikes your family, God is there to offer comfort, strength, wisdom, and love. When you don't feel like praying, take time to pray anyway. I heard it said once, "that it's the times when you don't feel like praying that you need to pray the most."

Start each day with a prayer before you even get out of bed and pray throughout the day. Pray while you are singing and pray while you are working. I used to have a plaque on the wall in my hallway that read, "A Family that Prays Together, Stays Together." Take time to pray with your family daily. Thank God for the food and shelter that He has provided for you. Thank Him for your salvation and for His unconditional love toward you and others. When you are praising God in prayer, there is no room for Satan in your heart. There have been days when I have left prayer out of my day, and my attitude was horrible all day long. When I start my day with God, I have an attitude of gratitude all day long.

PRAISE HIM IN CHOICES.

Think of all God has done for you. He loves you so much that He gave His only Son to die for your eternal salvation. He also forgives us when we mess up. He loves us so much that He doesn't want us to go without the things we need. He has a plan for our lives that gives hope and fulfillment in all that we do. When I think of all the times that He has protected me from harm and all the times that He has forgiven me for bad choices, I can't help but praise His holy name! To show gratitude in my attitude is to re-commit my life to Him daily. In all that I say and in all that I do, I want to put Him first in my life. This is my way of showing God that I am grateful for the sacrifices that He has made on my behalf. I heard a youth minister speak years ago about how Satan loves it when we mess up and make choices that are in opposition to God. He said that he pictured Satan just laughing in God's face every time that happened. When I thought about that, it broke my heart. I never want Satan to have an opportunity to laugh at my God because of something I have done. I want to make choices daily that will please my God. Reading the Bible daily will equip us all to make godly choices. Start each day in God's word to ensure an attitude of gratitude.

In the space below, write a prayer to God thanking Him for all He has done for you. Ask Him to help you live your life with an attitude of gratitude daily.

_____

_____

_____

_____

_____

_____

_____

DAY 2
THANK GOD FOR TEACHERS!

Today, I would like to invite you to take a trip with me down Memory Lane. Let's go back to the earliest years we can remember and think about those men and women who took time to see the good in us when no one else did and believed in us, no matter what. Try and remember the people who saw potential in you and challenged you to live up to that potential. For me, most of these men and women were teachers. Is that true for you too?

Did you have any children in your classes who seemed to always raise their hand to answer every question or to tell some long and drawn out story when the teacher was trying to teach the class? Well, I must admit, I was that little girl. I always wanted to put my "two cents worth" in on every subject. Now that I think back on that, I'm sure my teachers didn't particularly like it, but they never seemed to show it. My husband tells a story about a time when he was in school and the teacher was teaching a health lesson. The main topic for the day was "colds" and what to do when you have one. Randy raised his hand with pride, and his teacher called upon him only to hear him say to the whole class, "I had a cold once!" at which time the entire class broke into laughter. His teacher did not

VERSES FOR THE DAY

As for you, Titus, promote the kind of living that reflects wholesome teaching. Teach the older men to exercise self-control, to be worthy of respect, and to live wisely. They must have sound faith and be filled with love and patience. Similarly, teach the older women to live in a way that honors God. They must not slander others or be heavy drinkers. Instead, they should teach others what is good. These older women must train the younger women to love their husbands and their children, to live wisely and be pure, to work in their homes, to do good, and to be submissive to their husbands. Then they will not bring shame on the word of God. In the same way, encourage the young men to live wisely. And you yourself must be an example to them by doing good works of every kind. Let everything you do reflect the integrity and seriousness of your teaching. Teach the truth so that your teaching can't be criticized. Then those who oppose us will be ashamed and have nothing bad to say about us. Slaves must always obey their masters and do their best to please them. They must not talk back or steal, but must show themselves to be entirely trustworthy and good. Then they will make the teaching about God our Savior attractive in every way. For the grace of God has been revealed, bringing salvation to all people. And we are instructed to turn from godless living and sinful pleasures. We should live in this evil world with wisdom, righteousness, and devotion to God, while we look forward with hope to that wonderful day when the glory of our great God and Savior, Jesus Christ, will be revealed. He gave his life to free us from every kind of sin, to cleanse us, and to make us his very own people, totally committed to doing good deeds. You must teach these things and encourage the believers to do them. You have the authority to correct them when necessary, so don't let anyone disregard what you say. Titus 2

humiliate him, but took his comment and turned it into a learning experience for the whole class. This was early in his life, but he has never forgotten it.

Teachers influence us more than we realize. I had a piano teacher in Plymouth, North Carolina, named Mrs. McClannahan. She loved teaching piano lessons and seemed to genuinely love teaching me to play the instrument. To this day when I think of her, I get a "warm fuzzy" and long to go back to her house for another lesson.

My husband and I were in a grocery store in Elberton, Georgia, a few years ago, and right there in the frozen foods section this rather large woman came running over to my husband and gave him a great big hug. I wasn't sure who she was, but I could tell she was a very special person who cared deeply about my husband. Once Randy was able to come up for air, he introduced me to his seventh grade teacher. It was teachers like this that helped shape us into the adults we are today!

My list of great teachers could go on for days. I am very grateful for each and every one of them!

In the space below, list a few of the teachers that you have fond memories of from your childhood.

_____

_____

_____

_____

Most teachers live very sacrificial lives. They not only teach the daily curriculum, but teach personal relationship skills. Oh, I know they get their summers off, but how many teachers do you know that actually do nothing in the summer? The teachers that I know are usually furthering their education or volunteering to teach Vacation Bible School or working in camps. Their love for children goes way beyond the classroom, and we need to have an attitude of gratitude for each of them. They certainly don't do it for the money, and the teachers that I know don't do it for the summer vacation either. They do it because they want to make a difference in the lives of others. When was the last time you showed your gratitude to a teacher?

In the space below, write a prayer to God thanking Him for the teachers who have influenced your life in positive ways.

_____

_____

_____

_____

_____

Another group of teachers that come to mind are those men and women who teach Sunday School. They volunteer week after week and with little or no recognition. So many of the values that have been instilled in me are a direct result of a Sunday School teacher. I learned the importance of memorizing scripture from Mrs. Styons and songs like "The B-I-B-L-E" and "Fishers of Men" from other Sunday School teachers. I am so grateful for those who took the instructions about teaching from God's word seriously.

The influence they had on me made an eternal difference!

We have so much to be thankful for, and we owe much of our success as adults to those who took an interest in us early on! Take time today to thank teachers for all they do!

DAY 3

A TRUE FRIEND IS A RARE FIND

VERSES FOR THE DAY

A friend is always loyal, and a brother is born to help in time of need.
Proverbs 17:17

There are "friends" who destroy each other, but a real friend sticks closer than a brother.
Proverbs 18:24

If you keep yourself pure, you will be a special utensil for honorable use. Your life will be clean, and you will be ready for the Master to use you for every good work. Run from anything that stimulates youthful lusts. Instead, pursue righteous living, faithfulness, love, and peace. Enjoy the companionship of those who call on the Lord with pure hearts.
2 Timothy 2:21-22

When I was in high school I had a group of girls that I associated myself with called the "crazy eight." We had a lot of the same interests and always seemed to be involved in the same activities. Within the group, I had different levels of friendships. I had my very best friends, my special friends, and those that I liked but didn't allow into the secret areas of my life. We all grew up, got married and have gone our separate ways. I thought we were friends, but actually we were more like social butterflies.

I have some true friendships that I have treasured for all of my adult life. We can go for months without seeing or talking to each other, and then when we do get together it is as if we have never been apart. A true friend loves you in spite of your failures. She wants the best for you and will hold you accountable when you are tempted to do something that is in opposition to God's plan for your life. She will take up for you when others are talking bad about you. She will be there when you are hurting. She will cry with you, laugh with you, encourage you, and chastise you. True friends are a rare find. If you have anyone that you consider to be this kind of friend, then you have a reason to have an attitude of gratitude!

Another sure sign of a true friend is one who wants what is best for you in every situation. Jealously and pettiness play no part in this type of friendship. If she sees you going down a path that will lead to destruction, she will be bold enough to say something to you. She will also want to bring out the best in you. She will encourage you to have a relationship with God.

When my children were small, I prayed a specific prayer to God asking Him to bring a friend into my life. I asked Him to give me a friend with children the same age as my children and a husband who had the same interests as my husband. One day Bobby came home from school and told me that he had a friend named David at school and he wanted to invite him over to play. I called his mother and introduced myself and told her that my son wanted to have her son over to play. We agreed to let them play together, and when she came by to pick up her son I knew this was the friend that I had prayed for. Her name was Connie. Her son was the same age as my son, she had a daughter who was the same age as my daughter, and our husbands had the same interests. It was truly a gift from God! We laughed together, cried together, and bonded in ways that only true friends should and do.

Over the course of the years, our lives began to drift apart. We moved to Nashville, Tennessee, and she and her family moved to Gainesville, Georgia. A few years ago, we received a phone call that their daughter had been killed in an automobile accident. One of the first things they thought about doing when they received the news of their daughter's death was to call us. Why? Because they knew that even though years and distance had separated us, we would still care as true friends do.

A true friend will take up for you when others criticize you. It is a good idea to shop for swimsuits with a true friend. They will keep you from making a purchase that you may regret later. They will understand when you are grumpy and lift you up when you are down. They will pray for you and pray with you. Even when they don't know what to say, they will be there for you.

If you have not yet found a true friend, write a prayer to God asking Him to send one your way. He will be faithful in doing so. If you have a true friend, write a prayer to God thanking Him for this gift from above.

_____

_____

_____

True friends are a rare find. To have an attitude of gratitude is to treat them the same way that they treat you!

DAY 4
AT LEAST I HAVE A JOB

VERSES FOR THE DAY

And now, dear brothers and sisters, we give you this command in the name of our Lord Jesus Christ: Stay away from all believers who live idle lives and don't follow the tradition they received from us. For you know that you ought to imitate us. We were not idle when we were with you. We never accepted food from anyone without paying for it. We worked hard day and night so we would not be a burden to any of you. We certainly had the right to ask you to feed us, but we wanted to give you an example to follow. Even while we were with you, we gave you this command: "Those unwilling to work will not get to eat." Yet we hear that some of you are living idle lives, refusing to work and meddling in other people's business. We command such people and urge them in the name of the Lord Jesus Christ to settle down and work to earn their own living. As for the rest of you, dear brothers and sisters, never get tired of doing good.
2 Thessalonians 3:6-13

Pay careful attention to your own work, for then you will get the satisfaction of a job well done, and you won't need to compare yourself to anyone else. For we are each responsible for our own conduct.
Galatians 6:4-5

Do you have a job? Are you gainfully employed? In the past few years, more and more companies are closing their doors or cutting back their workforce, leaving men and women without jobs. Yet those of us who have jobs don't always appreciate what we have until it is gone.

I have a friend who wanted to make a career move in her mid-forties. She had a good job but felt it was time to move in a different direction. We prayed daily that God would provide a better job opportunity for her. Then one day, out of the blue, she received a phone call from a friend from church telling her about a company that needed to fill a brand new position that required many of the skills and talents she possessed. She went through the lengthy interview process, and we continued praying for her. It finally happened; she was offered the job! She even received a higher salary! Needless to say, she accepted their offer and began a new career. Not long after she began, I started hearing her complain about the job. Once again, she was unsatisfied. Why? I believe that she had a lapse in memory and simply forgot that this job opportunity was an answered prayer, a gift from God, and a perfect match for her abilities.

The unemployment office has a steady stream of people who are longing for opportunities to work, yet those of us who have jobs are complaining about the fact that we "have to work."

There is not a perfect job situation anywhere. Do you know why? Because any time that you have more than one person involved in any project there will be conflict. Another reason is that 90% of all problems stem from a lack of communication. People are not all alike, and when you work outside the home you will find that not everyone will appreciate you for who you really are. Others will not have the same work ethic as you.

If you are working just to get a paycheck, then you need an attitude adjustment!

Years ago, I began praying that God would use me every day in every way. I said things to Him in my prayers like, "Lord, use me." "Help me to make a difference in the lives of others." "I'll go where you want me to go and do what you want me to do." In doing this, I have taken a different approach to my daily life. I truly believe that every job I have had is a direct result of these prayers. I must admit that I too have found myself complaining about the jobs, the people, the circumstances, the long hours, and the inconveniences. Shame on me when this happens!

In order to have a better attitude and to maintain it, I do the following:

1. Remind myself daily that the job is a way to make a living, but it is not my life.
2. Remind myself daily that God has placed me in this job to make a difference in the lives of others.
3. Remind myself daily that as a Christian I need to have a Christ-like attitude in everything I do.
4. Remind myself daily to treat everyone with dignity and respect even if they don't do the same for me.
5. Remind myself daily to spend my time, talents, and money earned in a way that pleases God.

When God blesses you with a job, use it to bless others!

Work willingly at whatever you do, as though you were working for the Lord rather than for people.
Colossians 3:23

When you have the mindset that you work for God in everything that you do, situations that seemed intolerable become more tolerable. You will begin to look at people through God's eyes and not through your own.

Try to find humor in each day! Laughter is good for you!

In the space below, write a prayer to God asking Him to help you keep an attitude of gratitude at work. Thank Him for providing you with gainful employment.

_____

_____

In the space below, list the good things about your job; then thank God for blessing you in so many ways.

_____

_____

_____

DAY 5

THE VALUE OF A CHURCH FAMILY

Have you accepted Christ as your Savior? Have you been obedient to Him in baptism? If so, who is responsible for teaching, leading, and guiding you in these important steps in your life?

For some it was their parents, friends, Sunday School teachers, pastors, or a co-worker. For others it may have been an author's book, a writer's song, or a touching movie.

In the space below, list the people or events that influenced you to learn more about Christ and to accept Him as your Savior.

_____

_____

_____

Have you heard the expression, "I'd rather see a sermon than to hear one any day"?

VERSES FOR THE DAY

I want you to know how much I have agonized for you and for the church at Laodicea, and for many other believers who have never met me personally. I want them to be encouraged and knit together by strong ties of love. I want them to have complete confidence that they understand God's mysterious plan, which is Christ himself. In him lie hidden all the treasures of wisdom and knowledge. I am telling you this so no one will deceive you with well-crafted arguments. For though I am far away from you, my heart is with you. And I rejoice that you are living as you should and that your faith in Christ is strong. And now, just as you accepted Christ Jesus as your Lord, you must continue to follow him. Let your roots grow down into him, and let your lives be built on him. Then your faith will grow strong in the truth you were taught, and you will overflow with thankfulness. Don't let anyone capture you with empty philosophies and high-sounding nonsense that come from human thinking and from the spiritual powers of this world, rather than from Christ. For in Christ lives all the fullness of God in a human body. So you also are complete through your union with Christ, who is the head over every ruler and authority. Colossians 2:1-10

Some of the most influential people in my life were those who walked the walk and didn't just talk the talk. They were role models for Christianity. They practiced integrity, humility, and concern for others in everything they did. They were real people with real problems. The difference was that they based their lives on God's word and set a Christ-like example for others to follow. They were not hung up on what other people would think about them. They lived their lives to please God. As I look back over my life, I can think of men and women as well as boys and girls who led by example. They took time to care about others in hopes that they could be instrumental in leading them to a relationship with Christ.

If you have not yet accepted Christ as your Savior, think of those around you who are setting the right examples for you to follow and get to know them. If they are sincere about their relationship with Christ, they will gladly answer any questions you may have for them.

I am grateful for every person who took time to love me and show me a glimpse of Christ's love through their actions. It is people like that who have convinced me that the Christian life is a life worth living. Because of this, my attitude should be the same. Out of gratitude for what I have, I should now influence others in the same way.

You don't have to be perfect to bring someone to Christ. You just have to be willing to allow God to use you. To have an attitude of gratitude in this area, simply be a friend to others. Provide help when help is needed. Share your experiences with others. Treat everyone with dignity and respect. Don't cast judgment on them; be a friend and show an interest in the things that interest them. Be sincere, available, and trustworthy.

Another way to show gratitude for your salvation and for those who influenced you is by getting involved in a local church. It is a support group in difficult times, a place for encouragement when you are feeling down, and a family like no other.

I value my church family! In this transient world that we live in, most people are working and living away from their blood relatives. The church family can serve as your family away from home. In some instances, the church family is stronger and more stable than the biological family unit that you may have experienced. They are there to catch you when you fall. They help you get back on your feet again and hold you accountable in your daily activities. The leaders have sacrificed in many ways to serve and teach the members of the church family. They care for those who are hurting and they comfort the sick. They give of their time for the sake of Christ 24/7. We should take time each week to acknowledge our gratitude toward them for all they do. It is out of a love they have for others that they do the things they do. They don't do it for recognition, but as human beings, I'm sure they would appreciate a "thank you" from time to time.

In the space below, write a prayer to God asking Him to bless the leaders of your church family and to show you ways to encourage them.

_____

_____

_____

_____

An attitude of gratitude toward others is to have an attitude of gratitude toward God. It is a true reflection of where you stand on matters of the heart!

HOLIDAY PLANNING
NOVEMBER
WEEK 1

Christmas cards may be purchased early in November. However, the best time to purchase them is right after Christmas. Most card shops will offer them for 50% off the original price. Then you can store them for the upcoming year.

It is best to get your Christmas cards signed, sealed and ready for delivery by the second week in November. Once Thanksgiving Day is over and the Christmas holiday begins, our schedules tend to fill up fast and it becomes much harder to find the time.

Set up a Christmas card station with pens, stamps, cards, and addresses. As you are working on the cards, play some Christmas music and light a holiday scented candle. Better yet, watch one of your favorite Christmas movies. Before you know it, the cards are ready for delivery!

TO DO LIST

Thanksgiving Plans:

____ Finalize travel plans for Thanksgiving.

____ Make a list of food items that you will prepare for Thanksgiving Day dinner.

____ Gather recipes and start your shopping list for baking and cooking supplies.

Christmas Plans:

____ Make a list of people to receive Christmas cards.

____ Purchase cards or begin working on your annual family newsletter.

____ Make an appointment with a photographer for the holiday family photograph.

____ Start forming your gift-giving list.

PERFECT CORN PUDDING

1 can cream-style corn
2 eggs, beaten
2 tablespoons flour
½ cup milk
½ cup sugar
2 tablespoons margarine

Melt butter in a 1½ quart casserole dish. Mix flour with milk until
smooth. After combining all ingredients, pour into the casserole dish.
Bake at 375° for about 45 minutes.

*(This has been one of my favorite dishes since I was a little girl. Hope
you enjoy!)*

SWEET POTATO CASSEROLE

3 cups mashed sweet potatoes
1 cup sugar
2 eggs, beaten
1 teaspoon vanilla
1 stick margarine
⅓ cup milk

Mix together potatoes, sugar, eggs, vanilla, margarine and ⅓ cup milk.
Put in 1½ quart casserole dish.

TOPPING

1 cup brown sugar
½ cup flour
⅓ stick margarine
1 cup chopped pecans

Mix topping ingredients together until crumbly and sprinkle evenly
over sweet potatoes. Bake at 350° until brown on top.
Remove from oven and cover with aluminum foil until cool.

(When I think of Thanksgiving dinner, I always think of sweet potato casserole.)

HOT CINNAMON APPLE CIDER

1 gallon of old-fashioned apple cider

Red hot candies

Place cider and ¼ cup of red hots in crock pot/slow cooker.

Serve warm.

(Permeates your home with a holiday fragrance and tastes delicious!)

DAILY TO DO LIST:

Sunday: _____

_____

_____

Monday: _____

_____

_____

Tuesday: _____

_____

_____

Wednesday: _____

_____

_____

Thursday: _____

_____

_____

Friday: _____

_____

_____

Saturday: _____

_____

_____

PEOPLE TO RECEIVE CARDS:

_____

_____

_____

_____

_____

_____

_____

_____

_____

_____

_____

_____

_____

_____

_____

_____

_____

_____

_____

_____

_____

GROUP SESSION

WEEK 1

ATTITUDE OF GRATITUDE

Following the arrival activity time, start the group sessions by reading the introduction page and then open the lesson with prayer.

PRAISE THE LORD!

Have someone read the scripture aloud. Spend some time discussing what it means to praise the Lord. Then ask the members to give examples of ways they praise God through song, prayer, and choices. Ask them to talk about things in the lessons that may have given them a reason to praise the Lord with a new outlook and approach.

THANK GOD FOR TEACHERS!

Have someone read the scripture aloud. Encourage the members to take a trip down Memory Lane and tell others about a teacher who touched them in a positive way during their childhood. (Let this be a fun time of sharing!) Give them an opportunity to tell funny stories and laugh about their past.

A TRUE FRIEND IS A RARE FIND

Have someone read the scripture aloud. Take time to discuss the definition of a "true" friend. In order to have a true friend, one must invest time in the relationship. Encourage the members to come up with creative ways to keep a friendship alive and to show their friend how much they appreciate them.

AT LEAST I HAVE A JOB

Have someone read the scripture aloud. Ask the members to talk about things from the lesson that may have given them a reason to appreciate their job. Review the five (5) steps to maintaining a better attitude toward the job.

THE VALUE OF A CHURCH FAMILY

Have someone read the scripture aloud. Take time to celebrate your church family. Encourage the members to take some time throughout the week to express their attitude of gratitude to those in the church who make an eternal difference in the lives of others.

Review NOVEMBER WEEK 1 of the Holiday Planning guide.

Conclusion.

# WEEK 2

AVOIDING FAMILY FEUDS

There's no place like home for the holidays. Or is there? When you think about the family getting together for Thanksgiving or Christmas, do you see visions of bickering relatives? Are you already planning your way of escape? It doesn't have to be this way. Instead of dreading the days ahead with certain family members, take time to prepare for the occasion and do everything that is possible on your part to avoid family feuds.

In this second week of study, we will look into God's word and discover ways to deal with relatives. We will also seek ways to learn from the family and appreciate the relatives that God has placed in our lives.

Anticipate all that God wants to teach you this week! Ask Him to show you the things He wants you to see every day as you study His word. Be open to a fresh new approach to life!

DAY 1
Coping with
Clashing Kin

DAY 2
Who Are
You Trying
to Please
Anyway?

DAY 3
Don't Wear
Out Your
Welcome

DAY 4
You Are a
Grownup
Now

DAY 5
Forget About
It!

DAY 1
COPING WITH CLASHING KIN

Don't copy the behavior and customs of this world, but let God transform you into a new person by changing the way you think. Then you will learn to know God's will for you, which is good and pleasing and perfect. Romans 12:2

Don't just pretend to love others. Really love them. Hate what is wrong. Hold tightly to what is good. Love each other with genuine affection, and take delight in honoring each other. Romans 12:9-10

Never pay back evil with more evil. Do things in such a way that everyone can see you are honorable. Do all that you can to live in peace with everyone. Romans 12:17-18

Don't let evil conquer you, but conquer evil by doing good. Romans 12:21

Have you noticed that it is easier to treat a stranger with respect than it is a family member? Why is that? It can be a real challenge to deal with relatives without feeling hurt or misunderstood. This is a frustration that most adults face within their families. So if you are experiencing these feelings, you are not alone. According to Leonard Felder, Ph.D., author of *When Difficult Relatives Happen to Good People* (Rodale, 2003), 68% of us approach holiday get-togethers with feelings of dread or obligation.

There are some members of the family who think they are just showing concern for others by the comments they make, but for some reason the way they express themselves pushes buttons inside of us that cause anger, hurt feelings, or defensive comments to come out in retaliation.

Place a check by the comments or questions below you sometimes hear at family get-togethers that cause you to experience feelings of anger, frustration, or hurt.

____ "How much weight have you gained anyway?"

____ "Are you ever going to get a better paying job?"

____ "What's wrong with you? Why can't you find someone to marry you?"

____ "Don't you ever make your kids behave?"

____ "She's just like her Daddy. She'll never amount to anything."

____ "Why can't you be more like your sister?"

____ "I tried to teach you better than that, and you still haven't learned after all these years."

___ "We tried to tell you not to marry him and you wouldn't listen!"

___ "She can't help it."

___ "If you worked as hard as they do, you might have nicer things too."

___ "The way you act is an embarrassment to this family!"

___ "If she had been the first child, I can assure you that we would not have had other children. She was such a bad child!"

___ "Don't you know how to clean your house? I thought I taught you better."

___ "Your kids are spoiled rotten."

___ "Have you looked in the mirror lately? I don't think you need another piece of cake!"

As you checked off some of these comments or questions, did you begin to experience feelings of anger, frustration, or hurt?

In the space below, write a prayer to God asking Him to help you find ways to deal with the negative comments differently this holiday season.

_____

_____

_____

If you have experienced negative feelings at family get-togethers in the past, then I want to offer some solutions that will make this year better for you.

Lighten Up! Try not to take the negative comments so personally. Your family members usually think they are being helpful by making observations about your love life, work life, or weight. Don't feel obligated to defend the questions or comments. You did that last year and the year before and the year before and the year before. Why not approach this year differently?

Most family members are predictable and will say and do the same things every year. Before you leave home or before they come to visit, whichever the case may be, jot down the things that you think will happen and prepare yourself mentally to respond without being defensive. Ask God to help you understand that for some family members this is their way of showing you that they care and love you. Learn to laugh about it, and accept the fact that some people will never change. However, you can change how you respond to them and set a better tone for the once dreaded family get-together!

There is no need to compete! Getting together with the family should not be a time for competition. Be glad for those who have success in their adult lives. Offer encouragement and let them know that you are proud of their accomplishments. If they have a bigger house, better car, or a fatter checkbook, be happy for them. Try not to be jealous of them, but thank God for their blessings. If your siblings start bragging about their successes, don't feel obligated to defend the reasons that you may be lagging behind. If you begin to feel overwhelming jealousy, leave the room and begin to pray. Take time to be reminded once again of all the blessings you have, and remember that "stuff" is not what life is all about. Enjoy the nice things your family members might have, but don't let the fact that they have more than you take away your joy.

If you are the family member that has the nicer things, don't brag about it. Instead, share it with others and open up your home to them, drive your car to the mall, and be generous with others. If you sense that others are jealous of you, pray that God will show you ways to keep this from happening.

A plan of escape...Sometimes even your best attempts at getting along with the family will be defeated. When you see this happening, why not plan to escape for a few hours by sneaking off to the movies. You can also volunteer to make a run to the grocery store for some last-minute items. Another plan of escape that also serves as a really good stress release is a fast walk around the neighborhood. Just because you are home for the holidays doesn't mean you have to spend every single minute with your relatives. Slipping off for some time alone with God will do wonders for your overall attitude and will enable you to avoid family feuds.

Remember when you were a child and you were able to go outside and play? Well, you still can! Instead of spending time on pins and needles hoping to avoid family feuds, why not play board games, horseshoes, volleyball, card games, flag football, or just spend time with the children doing what they love to do. Make this holiday get-together one that everyone enjoys. Monopoly was the game of choice for my children growing up. Every holiday they looked forward to seeing their cousins and playing this game. They are all adults now, and they still talk about the fun they had each year playing together. Last Thanksgiving, we had a great time singing along with the karaoke machine. The adults and children alike had a blast.

RECIPE FOR AVOIDING FAMILY FEUDS

Find ways to keep your sense of humor!
Be thankful for the different personalities!
Let the negative comments roll off your back!
Choose to make the best of the time you have together!
Pray....Pray...Pray!

DAY 2

WHO ARE YOU TRYING TO PLEASE ANYWAY?

VERSES FOR THE DAY

So be careful how you live. Don't live like fools, but like those who are wise. Make the most of every opportunity in these evil days. Don't act thoughtlessly, but understand what the Lord wants you to do.
Ephesians 5:15-17

Live wisely among those who are not believers, and make the most of every opportunity. Let your conversation be gracious and attractive so that you will have the right response for everyone.
Colossians 4:5-6

Give thanks to the Lord, for he is good! His faithful love endures forever.
Psalm 136:1

"Honor your father and mother. Then you will live a long, full life in the land the Lord your God is giving you."
Exodus 20:12

Have you noticed that some people are impossible to please? I have friends who have said to me many times that no matter how hard they tried, there was just no way to ever please their parents. They seemed to be motivated by fear in many instances. If they did not bring home a report card with all "A's," they knew they would be punished. If they played sports, they had to be the captain of the winning team or their parents called them failures. It's not always the parents that are hard to please. Sometimes it is an older brother or sister, an uncle or aunt, or a grandparent. There are different reasons for this harsh motivation. I have discovered that most of the time these critical people are simply trying to live out their unfulfilled dreams through someone else. They are trying to teach others to be the perfect person they aren't or to justify their own mistakes and life choices. When you can come to grips with this in your own life, it will be easier to accept the fact that it is okay if you don't please them all of the time.

I know women who refuse to spend time with their family members because they never feel they will measure up to their expectations. Being in their presence causes feelings of anxiety and inadequacies, so they conveniently find other things to do during the holidays. That way, they don't have to feel that they have disappointed the family again.

Criticism is not easy to hear. Especially when you have done everything to the best of your ability. Today we are going to take a new and improved approach toward avoiding family feuds.

In the space below, answer this question: Who should you be trying to please?

GOD

It is impossible to please everyone. Even if you have done your best to make sure that everyone around you is happy, someone will complain. If you are the hostess for the family get-together and people complain about the meal being served too late, or the food being too cold, or the music is too loud, or that you ran out of gravy before they got any, take a deep breath and ask yourself this question: "Who am I trying to please anyway?"

As you go through the holidays, remember that the only person you need to please is God. In the space below, write a prayer to God asking Him to help you remember that He is the only person you need to try and please.

If you live your life in a way that pleases God, everything else will fall into place. The attitude that you have toward the complainers will be different. You will feel energized about serving others (even if they grumble the whole time) because you are doing something that pleases God. Some people seem to think they were put on the earth to make other people's lives miserable. Love those people and understand that your happiness does not depend on whether they are pleased with you. Your happiness, joy, and contentment come from God being pleased with you.

In the space below, write the words of scripture found in Philippians 3:13.

Brothers, I do not consider that I have made it on my own. But one thing I do: forgetting what lies behind and straining forward to what lies ahead.

In order to live a life that pleases God, it is important to spend time reading the Bible and in prayer. There are practical ways of living taught throughout His word. When you begin to live your life for Him and no one else, the criticism will not affect you in the same way. Measure every criticism with what God says and strive to measure up to His expectations. He loves everyone with an unconditional love. Even when we mess up, and all of us mess up from time to time, He will still be there to encourage, build up, and love us always!

DAY 3

DON'T WEAR OUT YOUR WELCOME

My dad, Gene McGhee, was a very optimistic person. He didn't live an easy life, but in spite of his struggles he always found reasons to laugh. He was known for his corny jokes. He died at the age of 47, and on his deathbed he was still trying to make people laugh. He used many funny anecdotes that I am reminded of during the holidays. When he would finish a meal, he would push his plate away and say, "Thank you for that meal; I have just had a gentile sufficiency." He loved to entertain, and we had guests in our home quite often. An old-fashioned term for guests is "company." Have you ever heard the expression, "We're having company over for dinner"? My dad used to laugh and say that the definition of "company" is to tell someone to make themselves at home when you wish they really were. You might have to think about that one for a minute. How long should you stay for a visit over the holidays? Three days is a good rule when planning your holiday visits. This length of time allows the family to enjoy your company, but not feel worn out from the stay. Whether you are the guest or the hostess, the cost of the visit begins to take a toll on the pocketbook after three days.

Even if you are going to visit your parents, remember that since you have moved out they have other activities and schedules to keep. The older your parents get, the more set in their ways they will become. I've heard parents say, "It was great to see them come but even better to see them go!" Try not to overextend your welcome. This will minimize the chances for a family feud. It is better to leave before the hostess wants than to have them celebrate when you finally leave.

Another way to wear out your welcome is to walk in and plop yourself down on the sofa as if you have been declared "queen for the day." Some hostesses prefer that you stay out of the kitchen, and if that is the case in your family then you should respect their wishes. However, there are other things that need to be done throughout the day. As a courtesy, even if you know you are not going to be needed in the kitchen, volunteer to assist with preparing the drinks, setting up places for the children, taking out the trash, or setting the table. Preparing a special holiday meal usually involves many hours of preparation. For some cooks it takes days, and by the time the meal is actually served they are exhausted. Why not offer to clean up after the meal while the hostess escapes to the bedroom for a nap?

VERSES FOR THE DAY

Rejoice in our confident hope. Be patient in trouble, and keep on praying. When God's people are in need, be ready to help them. Always be eager to practice hospitality.
Romans 12:12-13

Cheerfully share your home with those who need a meal or a place to stay.
1 Peter 4:9

Near the shore where we landed was an estate belonging to Publius, the chief official of the island. He welcomed us and treated us kindly for three days.
Acts 28:7

It can be so much fun to spend time with the family during the holidays. If you will be visiting relatives that live out of town, one way to make the visit fun for everyone is to share in the responsibilities. This way the hostess does not feel overwhelmed about providing all the meals.

A friend of mine shared the following idea with me. I loved it, and with her permission, I now share it with others. Each year she hosts the family get-together at Thanksgiving. Her parents will arrive a few days before the rest of the family. The rest of the family consists of adult siblings and their spouses and children. Each day a different family is in charge of preparing the meals, clean up, and the expense. My friend prepares everything on Thanksgiving Day. This allows everyone to enjoy the holiday visit, including the hostess. She assigns each family a different day to own the kitchen, and they all know in advance what is expected.

In the space below, list other ways that the family members may share in the responsibilities of the holiday get-together.

_____

_____

_____

Dining out can get pricey, so why not get creative in the meal preparation by allowing others into the kitchen during the visit and hopefully everyone can push their empty plates away and say, "I just had a gentile sufficiency!"

In the space below, write a prayer to God asking Him for guidance as you plan for the upcoming holiday season. Ask Him to show you ways to prevent wearing out your welcome.

_____

_____

_____

One of my favorite movies is *Christmas Vacation*. If you aren't sure what it means to "wear out your welcome," then rent this movie and you'll see many examples of how this happens to the Griswalds. I venture to guess that most of us have some family members like the ones portrayed in this movie. Instead of feuding with the family, learn to enjoy the many differences among your kin!

DAY 4
YOU ARE A GROWNUP NOW

Do you find that you revert to your childhood days when you come together with the family? If you are the youngest of the siblings, do you allow the older brothers and sisters to boss you around? If you are the oldest, do you catch yourself telling your younger siblings what to do? When your parents are around, do you allow them to manipulate you into feeling guilty if you tell your son he does not have to eat the green beans? This could very well be the reason for some of the frustrations that you experience when you gather with the family for the holidays. By dealing with your family as an adult—not as a child—you'll keep a balance and avoid family feuds.

In the space below, write a prayer to God asking Him to keep you from reverting back to your childhood days when you come together with the family.

_____

_____

_____

When you are at a family gathering, take time to observe the behavior of others. This may be a perfect opportunity for you to learn more about how you don't want to behave with your spouse, children, or friends. You may have been raised in a home where yelling and endless arguing took place and was considered to be acceptable behavior. Now that you are grown and have a family of your own, you have decided to handle things differently through calm discussion. You may have come from a household that did not choose to say a prayer of thanksgiving before eating a meal. As a grownup, you have chosen to begin each meal with prayer.

VERSES FOR THE DAY

May God our Father and the Lord Jesus Christ give you grace and peace.
Philippians 1:2

For I fully expect and hope that I will never be ashamed, but that I will continue to be bold for Christ, as I have been in the past. And I trust that my life will bring honor to Christ, whether I live or die.
Philippians 1:20

With the Lord's authority I say this: Live no longer as the Gentiles do, for they are hopelessly confused. Their minds are full of darkness; they wander far from the life God gives because they have closed their minds and hardened their hearts against him. They have no sense of shame. They live for lustful pleasure and eagerly practice every kind of impurity. But that isn't what you learned about Christ.
Ephesians 4:17-20

Carefully determine what pleases the Lord.
Ephesians 5:10

My son, pay attention to my wisdom; listen carefully to my wise counsel. Then you will show discernment, and your lips will express what you've learned.
Proverbs 5:1-2

In the space below, list changes that you have implemented in your family as an adult that differ from those of your childhood.

_____

_____

_____

As an adult, you have choices to make—choices on how you will interact with your spouse, children, friends, and co-workers. You have a choice to make as to where you and your family will attend church. You also have to choose a career path that suits you and the needs of your family. As children come along, more choices need to be made such as where they will attend school and whom their playmates will be. Decisions, decisions, decisions! When you make these decisions, not everyone will agree with them. It's okay! Everyone makes mistakes along the way, but if you are doing what you feel is best for you and your family then feel good about it.

Seek wisdom from God and ask Him to direct your path. By dealing with your family as an adult, you can feel more confident in the relationships and friendships that may develop with siblings and parents.

In the space below, write the words found in Philippians 4:13.

I can do everything Through him who gives me Strength.

_____

God has promised to be with His children through thick and thin. When I first became an adult, I relied on my biological father for everything. I didn't make a decision without calling him. I valued his opinion and was convinced that he would never lead me astray. He was right most of the time, but early in my adult life my father passed away. The person I depended on to help me with life's challenges was gone. It was then that I accepted my role as a grownup and turned to the One who would never leave me and would always have the right advice in every situation. Some of the most critical people we encounter are those we call relatives. With God by your side you can walk into the next family get-together with God-confidence. It outweighs self-confidence in every way!

> For I can do everything through Christ, who gives me strength.
> Philippians 4:13

I'm so glad I'm a part of the family of God!

DAY 5
FORGET ABOUT IT!

VERSES FOR THE DAY

You were dead because of your sins and because your sinful nature was not yet cut away. Then God made you alive with Christ, for he forgave all our sins. He canceled the record of the charges against us and took it away by nailing it to the cross.
Colossians 2:13-14

Make allowance for each other's faults, and forgive anyone who offends you. Remember, the Lord forgave you, so you must forgive others.
Colossians 3:13

Don't worry about anything; instead, pray about everything. Tell God what you need, and thank him for all he has done. Then you will experience God's peace, which exceeds anything we can understand. His peace will guard your hearts and minds as you live in Christ Jesus.
Philippians 4:6-7

Some of the worst pain and the deepest hurt that anyone experiences come from those in the family. I have seen children suffer greatly at the hands of their parents. I know women who have difficulties in relationships of all kinds because of the trauma faced as a young girl. Hurtful feelings that cut deep into the soul may tear families apart. For some, the pain is hidden away or covered up by humor. Others hide behind excessive weight, promiscuous lifestyles, or hatred toward those who allowed such things to go on in the family. It doesn't matter what degree of pain you are experiencing. I will offer you the same advice for handling it. As you get ready to face another family gathering, it's time to forget about it and move on.

Whatever caused you such pain is in the past and can't harm you now unless you choose to allow it to paralyze you. There was a time in my life when I was allowing a hurt from my past to ruin every family get-together we had. I would attend the event complaining to my husband before going and let everyone around me know that I was there only out of obligation. I arrived angry and left angry. I dreaded being around this person and was determined not to enjoy myself. I was miserable and did my best to make sure everyone else was miserable too. One Sunday morning, I sat under a very wise teacher and dear friend who spoke on the topic of forgiveness, and I knew I had some soul searching to do. I knew the importance of forgiving others, but I had become self-centered and had allowed myself to obsess over something that someone had done to me. I asked God to help me forgive and prayed earnestly to forget about the hurtful things that had occurred. With His help, I was able to do just that.

I want to invite you to take a journey with me. I pray that you will discover ways to forgive those family members who may have hurt you. In the space below, write a prayer asking God to show you how to forgive others.

_____

_____

_____

What has God done for you?

_____

_____

What has He done with the charges against you?

_____

_____

What should you do to the person that offends you?

_____

What did the Lord do for you?

_____

Pray like this: Our Father in heaven, may your name be kept holy. May your Kingdom come soon. May your will be done on earth, as it is in heaven. Give us today the food we need, and **forgive** *us our sins, as we have* **forgiven** *those who sin against us. And don't let us yield to temptation, but rescue us from the evil one. "If you* **forgive** *those who sin against you, your heavenly Father will* **forgive** *you. But if you refuse to* **forgive** *others, your Father will not* **forgive** *your sins."*
Matthew 6:9-15

How does Jesus ask God to forgive us our sins?

_____

What will our heavenly Father do for us if we forgive others?

_____

_____

What happens if we refuse to forgive others?

_____

_____

If you want to put the past in the past, you must forgive the offense. It will not be easy and won't necessarily happen quickly, but the freedom that you will experience once you let go is indescribable! When I forgave the person in my family, I began to enjoy the get-togethers more than ever before. Only you can choose to forgive those who hurt you. You might not see a change in the other person, but the change that will come over you will be full of peace, joy, and contentment.

In the space below, write a prayer asking God to help you forgive the way He instructs us to in His word.

_____

_____

_____

Do you want to avoid family feuds? If so, you must forgive! Just like God does for us, we must forget about it!

Each time the old feelings overtake you, remember to do as it says in Philippians 4:8-9:

And now, dear brothers and sisters, one final thing. Fix your thoughts on what is true, and honorable, and right, and pure, and lovely, and admirable. Think about things that are excellent and worthy of praise. Keep putting into practice all you learned and received from me—everything you heard from me and saw me doing. Then the God of peace will be with you.

TO DO LIST

Thanksgiving Plans:

___ Purchase items on your shopping list for baking and cooking supplies.

___ Purchase turkey and ham.

___ Begin holiday baking.

Christmas Plans:

___ Write Christmas cards.

___ Budget your money for gift-giving.

___ Mark upcoming parties, dinners, get-togethers on your calendar.

___ Make plans to set aside a day on the calendar for baking with children.

SURVIVOR TIPS

Baskets make great gifts.

Bath – *soaps, bubble bath, a candle, washcloth, some soothing music.*

Reading – *bookmarks, magazines, devotional book, journal.*

Gardening – *seeds, garden tools, gloves, potted plants.*

Kitchen – *tea cups, specialty teas, napkins, towel, devotional book.*

Kids –*movies, teddy bear, children's praise music, children's books.*

When in doubt, food items make great gifts.

Fresh baked cinnamon rolls in a dish with a ribbon tied around it.

Breads – banana nut, sourdough, raisin and cinnamon, zucchini.

Line a basket with a colorful cloth. Fill with a variety of small breads.

Fill a holiday tin with Popcorn Scramble. *(Recipe on next page)*

Fill a jar with spiced pecans.

Fill a recipe box with some special "goodies."

Give homemade beverage mixes in unusual jars or crocks.

POPCORN SCRAMBLE

6 cups freshly popped popcorn
3 cups bite-sized rice cereal squares
1 cup ring-shaped puffed oat cereal
1 cup peanuts
½ cup margarine
1 cup firmly packed brown sugar
¼ cup light corn syrup
¼ teaspoon baking soda
1 teaspoon vanilla

Mix popcorn, cereal, and peanuts in a large bowl. Set aside.
Melt margarine in large saucepan. Stir in brown sugar and corn syrup.
Heat slowly, stirring constantly, to boiling. Cook without stirring 5 minutes.
Remove from heat. Stir in soda and vanilla. Drizzle over popcorn mixture.
Stir until well coated. Spoon into large shallow pan and bake for 1 hour in
pre-heated 250° oven. Stir several times.
*(My son, Bobby, loves Popcorn Scramble. It has been a tradition in our
home since 1985. Enjoy!)*

SPICED PECANS

2 cups pecan halves
1 cup sugar
5 tablespoons water
1 teaspoon vanilla
1 teaspoon cinnamon

In a saucepan bring the sugar, water, vanilla, and cinnamon to a boiling
point. Remove from heat. Stir in pecans, stir for 5 minutes.
Place on wax paper to dry.

HOLIDAY SPRITZER

1 gallon of white grape juice

2- liter bottle of ginger ale

Chill and serve in Christmas glasses.

DAILY TO DO LIST:

Sunday: _____

_____

_____

Monday: _____

_____

_____

Tuesday: _____

_____

_____

Wednesday: _____

_____

_____

Thursday: _____

_____

_____

Friday: _____

_____

_____

_____

Saturday: _____

_____

_____

PEOPLE TO RECEIVE CARDS:

_____

_____

_____

_____

_____

_____

_____

_____

_____

_____

_____

_____

_____

_____

_____

_____

_____

_____

_____

_____

_____

_____

_____

_____

_____

THANKSGIVING SHOPPING LIST:

_____

_____

_____

_____

_____

_____

_____

_____

_____

_____

_____

_____

_____

_____

_____

_____

_____

_____

_____

_____

_____

_____

_____

_____

GIFT-GIVING LIST:

_____

_____

_____

_____

_____

_____

_____

_____

_____

_____

_____

_____

_____

_____

TRAVEL ARRANGEMENTS:

_____

_____

_____

_____

_____

_____

_____

GROUP SESSION

WEEK 2

AVOIDING FAMILY FEUDS

Following the arrival activity time, start the group session by reading the introduction page and then open the lesson with prayer.

COPING WITH CLASHING KIN

Have someone read the scriptures aloud. Review the comments/questions that you sometimes hear at family get-togethers and encourage discussion about the feelings experienced. Ask the members what areas of this lesson caused them to re-think how they will respond to the clashing kin at this year's family get-together.

WHO ARE YOU TRYING TO PLEASE ANYWAY?

Have someone read the scriptures aloud, challenge the members to find ways to overcome the feeling of inadequacy that stems from trying to "measure up" by simply making a choice to focus on the importance of pleasing God above everyone and everything else around them. Have someone read page 36 aloud.

DON'T WEAR OUT YOUR WELCOME

Have someone read the scriptures aloud. Ask them to come up with some ways to prevent wearing out the welcome this year, whether it be guests coming to visit or being the guest of others.

YOU ARE A GROWNUP NOW

Have someone read the scriptures aloud. This is a tough subject for most. Spend some time discussing ways to avoid falling into the old traps of childhood in the adult years.

FORGET ABOUT IT!

This is a tough one! Start off with a prayer asking God to show each one in the class how to forgive others. Have someone read Colossians 2:13-14 aloud and then answer the questions on pages 45 and 46 as a group.

Review NOVEMBER WEEK 2 of the Holiday Planning guide.

Conclusion.

# WEEK 3

SAVE YOURSELF FROM HOLIDAY DEBT

Christmas comes but once a year, but after the gifts are opened the bills just keep on coming! Have you noticed that it is easy to justify a spending spree in the name of generosity? It is hard to resist applying for credit cards when the department store clerk asks, "Would you like to save 10% on your purchase today?" Of course I would like to save 10% on my purchase, but the catch comes when you say "yes." It means that in order to get the discount, you have to fill out a credit card application for that particular store.

Debt is a real struggle for many families in our society today. In this third week of study we will look at ways to break the credit card habit.

Anticipate all that God wants to teach you this week! Ask Him to show you the things He wants you to see every day as you study His word. Be open to a fresh new approach to life!

DAY 1
Making a List
and Checking
It Twice

DAY 2
Start Shopping
Now

DAY 3
Will That Be
Cash, Check,
or Credit?

DAY 4
I Made It
Myself!

DAY 5
Find a Mentor

DAY 1

MAKING A LIST AND CHECKING IT TWICE

If you start out on your holiday shopping spree without a gift-giving list, you may find yourself running out of cash before you complete your shopping. You may even run up on a fantastic sale of items that you have been wanting for some time, and end the day of shopping with bags of clothes for yourself, and nothing for family and friends. Your intentions were good, but the end result was bad. In some cases when this happens the cash flow is depleted, and you may feel that the only option left is to use credit cards.

Compulsive shopping can take a toll on the pocketbook. This is especially true when purchasing large items. Most furniture stores offer "no interest and no payments for an extended period of time." If you have not budgeted for these items, it is very tempting to fall into the debt trap. It is exciting to get new furniture; however, if you have not planned for it in your budget for the upcoming year, the purchase may cause financial worries that otherwise could have been avoided.

Make a list. If you do not include the following information on your list, you could still get to the store and spend more than you can honestly afford. Then the holiday debt begins.

What should you have on your list? The first step is to determine how much money you will spend. Once you have a set amount in mind then decide how much of that total amount you will spend on each person. This will enable you to shop with specific items in mind and keep you from gravitating toward the more expensive items in the store. Here is a sample of the type of things that should be included on the list.

Holiday Gift-Giving List – Not to Exceed $65.00

Name	Amount to Spend	*Gift Ideas	Amount Spent
Aunt Ruth	$15.00	Book, Scarf, Jewelry, Candle, Pillow	$11.72
Mom	$50.00	Coffee Maker, Sweater, Nightgown, Slippers, Purse	$49.98
	$65.00		**$61.70**

Once you decide how much to spend on each person, list different ideas that are in that price range and shop specifically for items listed. You may find that you are able to buy more than one of the items listed. Be frugal and stay within the limits that you set before leaving home!

Holiday Gift-Giving List – Not to Exceed $

Name	Amount to Spend	*Gift Ideas	Amount Spent
	$		$

DAY 2

START SHOPPING NOW

VERSES FOR THE DAY

Send your grain across the seas, and in time, profits will flow back to you. But divide your investments among many places, for you do not know what risks might lie ahead. When clouds are heavy, the rains come down. Whether a tree falls north or south, it stays where it falls. Farmers who wait for perfect weather never plant. If they watch every cloud, they never harvest. Ecclesiastes 11:1-4

"Do to others whatever you would like them to do to you. This is the essence of all that is taught in the law and the prophets." Matthew 7:12

For everything there is a season, a time for every activity under heaven. Ecclesiastes 3:1

Last-minute shopping can be expensive, especially if you are looking for something specific. The best time to start shopping for the holidays is now. Many of the department stores are trying to entice early shoppers with great sales. Since you already have your gift-giving list ready, I would suggest that you start collecting sale papers and try and find the best bargains.

In the space below, write down the stores that have the items you plan to purchase on sale.

_____

_____

_____

Now circle the stores that have the best deals and make plans to shop there first.

Those who choose to wait until the last minute may find that they are in a panic because the items they were going to purchase are no longer available. For some people this will cause them to overspend and blow the budget. Right now the hottest items are still available and usually on sale.

A few years ago, I discovered "on-line shopping" and I love it! I try and get a wish list from my children around the first of November, and I begin searching on-line for the best deals. Some companies will offer free shipping as well as discounted prices. It's great for me because I can come home from work, put on my flannel pajamas and my warm fuzzy slippers, and experience hassle free shopping. I usually sip on a cup of hot tea and listen to Christmas music.

If I am buying a gift for a friend or family member who lives out of town, I simply have their gift wrapped and shipped to them. It saves gas for my car, time away from home, and money. Try it this year and see how you like it.

The day after Thanksgiving kicks off the official holiday shopping season. The stores are much more crowded, and the merchandise begins to get picked over. If you start your shopping now, you will find better deals and avoid the rush. If you enjoy the hustle and bustle of the After Thanksgiving Day Sales and have specific items on your list that stores advertised as early bird specials, then by all means, feel free to get up at the crack of dawn and wait in line for the store to open! You might find a bargain that saves you a tremendous amount of money. I have been known to participate in this exciting day of shopping and had a blast doing so. If you have never done it, let me caution you...it is not for the shopper who enjoys browsing. You must be the type of person who enjoys a good fight. Most of the people who stand in those lines at 5:30 a.m. crawled right out of bed and came to the store without their coffee; it is not always a pleasant experience.

Shopping for a long period of time causes me to work up an appetite. In order to avoid spending money on food, I pack a cooler for the day. I include a sandwich, fruit, yogurt and bottled water. When I begin to feel hungry I head for the car, drop off my bags, and take my lunch out of the cooler. Instead of eating in the car, I go back into the mall and find a safe and relaxing place to eat my lunch. This allows me to take some time to regroup and check off the items purchased on my list. It also enables me to rest for a few minutes. After lunch I feel energized and ready to let the shopping begin once again.

I try and finish all of my holiday shopping and gift-giving before Thanksgiving. This allows me to enjoy the festivities of the season without the added pressures of holiday shopping. Did you notice that I said, "I try"? I don't always succeed in this plan, but the years that I have accomplished it have been so much easier on the pocketbook and in every other way,

My husband and I have a tradition that we have carried on for several years now. On Christmas Eve we go out for a relaxing breakfast and then to a mall. We don't go to the mall because we have shopping to do. We go to watch all of the last-minute shoppers who rush to and fro trying to finish their gift-giving purchases before the stroke of midnight. We usually find a comfortable bench and spend time chatting and enjoying the hustle and bustle without the pressures that most others are experiencing. Will we see you there this year? If so, will you be relaxing on a bench or rushing around for last-minute purchases?

Stores that offer one-stop shopping can not only save you time but money too. These types of stores will sometimes accept coupons or offer free gift-wrapping. Try and take advantage of the free services offered throughout the holiday season. Stay within your budget and save yourself from holiday debt in every way.

Just imagine how much better you will feel if you go out to get your mail in January and you don't have to pull credit card bills out of the mailbox. Wouldn't it be refreshing to know now that the upcoming year can be free of holiday debt? Planning ahead and shopping early will enable you to experience that very thing!

SAVE YOURSELF FROM HOLIDAY DEBT BY SHOPPING EARLY!

DAY 3

WILL THAT BE CASH, CHECK OR CREDIT?

"How will you be paying today? With cash, a check or credit card?" Do these words sound familiar? Are you tempted to pull out the credit card when they ask this question? Even when you have the cash to pay, do you start thinking of reasons that you should charge it instead?

For some people, using credit cards for all purchases works best. They have learned to budget and pay the balance in full by the due date. If you are disciplined enough to pay in full each month, then you can save on finance charges. You also have the convenience of paying for all purchases at once. However, if you are not able to pay the balance in full, you run the risk of adding pressure to the budget for the upcoming months and taking on debt that your finances are not equipped to handle. Also, having the mindset that you will pay the balance when it comes due is risky if you live from paycheck to paycheck. What if the company that you work for suddenly decides to downsize and you find yourself without a job? How do you plan to pay your debt then? It is more convenient to use a credit card for the purchases, but is it the best method of payment? Only you can decide.

For others, it seems to work better if they write checks or use their debit cards when making their purchases. The funds are deducted from their checking account immediately, and they don't have the hassle of paying a credit card bill later. It is not as convenient to purchase items with a check because you have to slow down and actually fill in the information on the check. You also need to remember to document the purchase in the checkbook register whether writing a check or using the debit card. This will keep you from spending more money than you actually have available in your checking account and prevent overspending. It is essential to balance the checkbook ahead of time to ensure that all outstanding

VERSES FOR THE DAY

Greed brings grief to the whole family, but those who hate bribes will live.
Proverbs 15:27

Better to live humbly with the poor than to share plunder with the proud.
Proverbs 16:19

Don't be concerned about the outward beauty of fancy hairstyles, expensive jewelry, or beautiful clothes. You should clothe yourselves instead with the beauty that comes from within, the unfading beauty of a gentle and quiet spirit, which is so precious to God.
1 Peter 3:3-4

God showed how much he loved us by sending his one and only Son into the world so that we might have eternal life through him. This is real love—not that we loved God, but that he loved us and sent his Son as a sacrifice to take away our sins.
1 John 4:9-10

checks have cleared. Make sure that you are aware of the amount of money you have available to use ahead of time. If you are disciplined enough to handle this procedure, then this may be the best method of payment for you. Only you can decide.

Neither the charge method nor the check method works for me. With both of these methods, I find myself spending more than I should. I have learned that my best method of payment is to use cash. When I budget for a certain amount of money to spend and include only that amount in an envelope along with my shopping list, I shop until I run out of money and then go home. When I get home, I mark off the items purchased, and when I have more cash to use, I go back out and shop again. It's okay if I don't get everything at once. Sometimes I have to regroup and come up with other ideas that are more in line with my budget. Shopping with cash is also more convenient. The cashier rings up the purchase, I give them cash, and they give me a receipt and change, then I'm off to my next destination. It is so simple. I have no other records to keep, no other checks to write, and no worries about how I plan to pay off the debt.

Gift giving should be fun. I'm afraid that some people have taken the joy out of the process by trying to do more than they can honestly afford. Instead of enjoying the experience of giving, it has become a dreaded time of year. I want to encourage you to put the joy back into the process by spending only what you can afford and nothing more!

In the space below, write down your method of payment and how you plan to handle it.

_____

_____

_____

As for me and my wallet, we will be paying with cash!
Avoid the temptation of overspending with your credit card. Do leave home without it!

DAY 4
I MADE IT MYSELF!

Some of my favorite gifts to receive are homemade items from family and friends.

Just knowing that they took the time to create something just for me means so much! Have you ever thought about making your gifts? Before you buy a gift, ask yourself, "Would something less expensive or homemade be just as thoughtful and appropriate?"

As you look back at your original gift-giving budget, have you been trying to figure out ways to cut down on the spending even more? Well, making your gifts can do just that!

You might be thinking that you don't have a single creative bone in your body and there is no way you could make anything. Let's take some time now and do some brainstorming.

Look at the list below and see if anything sparks your interest.

- Sew aprons to use when grilling or to use in the kitchen.

- Sew cloth napkins.

- Homemade purses are always fun to make and fun to receive!

- Knit scarves for all of your friends. You can create really cool scarves with one simple stitch. Even a beginner can do this. I did this for friends after one knitting lesson!

- Do you like to bake? Give a gift certificate for the Dessert of the Month Club. Each month bake a dessert and deliver it to their office or home. If they live out of town, mail it to them.

- Homemade food items are always a big hit!

VERSES FOR THE DAY

She is energetic and strong, a hard worker. She makes sure her dealings are profitable; her lamp burns late into the night. Her hands are busy spinning thread, her fingers twisting fiber. She extends a helping hand to the poor and opens her arms to the needy. Proverbs 31:17-20

So I decided there is nothing better than to enjoy food and drink and to find satisfaction in work. Then I realized that these pleasures are from the hand of God. Ecclesiastes 2:24

I love you, Lord; you are my strength. The Lord is my rock, my fortress, and my savior; my God is my rock, in whom I find protection. He is my shield, the power that saves me, and my place of safety. I called on the Lord, who is worthy of praise, and he saved me from my enemies. Psalm 18:1-3

- There are a variety of woodwork projects that could be made. Things such as picture frames, tables, stools, or painted wall plaques.

- Paint a picture, sign it and have it framed.

Check out this week's Holiday Planning section for more ideas.

It may be that you are in a financial situation that does not allow for any spending this year. That's okay too! Even if you have no money, you may have services that you could give instead.

- Gift certificates for free babysitting for the weekend of their choice.

- Gift certificates for a home-cooked meal to be delivered on the night of their choice.

- Gift certificates for cleaning service for the room and time of their choice.

- Gift certificates for lawn care.

Giving a gift should be from the heart and not out of obligation. Since you are planning your holiday gift-giving early, there is time to make gifts for others. This is another way to save on holiday debt. Giving gifts should not be a competition but rather out of appreciation and love for others. What do you enjoy doing? Find ways to share your interests with others. When you take time to make a gift for someone special, you are truly giving from the heart. No one ever said that you had to buy a gift in order for it to be meaningful.

In the space below, list your homemade gift ideas and consider the cost.

_____

_____

_____

Check out your local craft stores. The amount of money spent on a gift is not what counts. It is the thought and effort put into it that matters most.

There are so many ways that you can show your appreciation for others without having to deplete funds in the bank account. As you go through this day, try and come up with ideas that suit you and your lifestyle.

Below is a list of some gifts that I have received through the years that were homemade, or services that were given to me and my family:

- Peanut brittle.
- Chocolate chip cookies in a cookie tin lined with a Christmas towel.
- Homemade Chinese dinner delivered to our home.
- Babysitting service.
- 30-minute massage.
- Homemade Italian spaghetti and sauce with meatballs.
- Duffle bag with picture of the church scanned on front.
- Homemade recipe book with favorite family recipes included.
- 5-bean soup mix in a decorative jar with recipe attached.
- Christmas bowl full of popped popcorn
- Homemade Christmas tree ornaments
- Lawn care
- Homemade hot chocolate mix

As you begin to create your own list, remember that the earlier you start making your gifts, the easier it will be. The more gifts you can make, the less gifts you will need to purchase.

Happy Holidays!

DAY 5
FIND A MENTOR

VERSES FOR THE DAY

A wise child accepts a parent's discipline; a mocker refuses to listen to correction.
Proverbs 13:1

My son, pay attention to my wisdom; listen carefully to my wise counsel. Then you will show discernment, and your lips will express what you've learned.
Proverbs 5:1-2

Don't worry about anything; instead, pray about everything. Tell God what you need, and thank him for all he has done. Then you will experience God's peace, which exceeds anything we can understand. His peace will guard your hearts and minds as you live in Christ Jesus.
Philippians 4:6-7

Do you have a frugal friend? Does she seem to have a good grasp on ways to avoid the dreaded holiday debt? If so, then ask her how it is done. Don't be afraid to admit that you need to work on some things in this area of your life. Ask her to help you learn where to find the best bargains. Take notes on how she handles persuasive sales clerks.

A wise person seeks help when help is needed. In the space below, write a prayer to God asking Him to provide you with a mentor.

_____

_____

When you find a mentor, ask her to show you how things are done. Invite her to go shopping with you, and to hold you accountable for your spending decisions. Changing your spending habits and your overall outlook toward debt will allow you to put joy and excitement back into the gift-giving process.

I am grateful for the mentors in my life. Godly women who have instructed me in areas of finance as well as domestic training through the years are very near and dear to my heart. I haven't always done things the right way, and there are times when I still find myself rushing around at the last minute trying to find a gift. However, for the most part I am on the right track. I am praying that you will receive guidance and direction as you seek to change your ways and avoid holiday debt!

As you prepare for the holidays, ask God to help you control your spending habits, and to give you the control needed to stay within your budget. Using cash instead of credit cards is a foreign concept for most Americans. If you have done things one way for so long, it can be difficult to see it any other way. I would like to recommend that you try a new way of shopping this year. If it doesn't work, go back to your old way next year.

Have a debt-free happy holiday season!

HOLIDAY PLANNING
NOVEMBER
WEEK 3

TO DO LIST

Christmas Plans:

___ Finish writing your Christmas cards.

___ Ask your family for their wish lists.

___ Begin shopping for holiday gifts.

___ Continue to bake goodies and freeze them.

___ Make plans for holiday parties and buy invitations.

SURVIVOR TIPS

For the hard-to-please people who have everything, a gift certificate to a restaurant, ice cream shop, or fast-food restaurant is always a hit.

Give a collection of your favorite recipes in an attractive binder or recipe box.

Wrap popcorn balls in clear plastic wrap. Tie with ribbon and jingle bells.

Tie a pretty bow around the handle of a plastic scoop that has been filled with candy, nuts, or mints and covered with plastic wrap.

Fresh flowers are a nice gift for those that are longing for warm weather and springtime.

If you have friends who are movie enthusiasts, gift certificates to movies are a real treat for them.

Gas prices have skyrocketed! Why not give a gift certificate for a tank of gas?

PUMPKIN DELIGHT

Crust: 1 yellow cake mix (reserve one cup for topping)
1 stick margarine, melted
1 egg

Filling: 1 can (29 ounces) pumpkin
2 eggs
$^2/_3$ cup milk
1 cup sugar
1 teaspoon cinnamon
½ teaspoon nutmeg
½ teaspoon ginger
½ teaspoon salt

Topping: 1 cup reserved cake mix
2 tablespoons sugar
½ stick margarine

Preheat oven to 350°.

To make the crust, combine cake mix (minus 1 cup), melted
margarine, and egg. Press into a greased 9x13 inch pan.
Combine all filling ingredients and mix until smooth. Pour over crust.
For topping, mix reserved cake mix, cinnamon, and sugar; cut in
margarine until crumbly. Sprinkle over filling.
Bake 50 minutes, or until knife inserted into center comes out clean.

SUPER BREAKFAST CASSEROLE

6 eggs
1 cup milk
6 ounces cheddar cheese (grated)
1 pound sausage or bacon
Frozen hash brown patties (box of 9)
Line a 9x13 inch glass baking dish with frozen hash browns. Sprinkle hash browns with fried, drained, and crumbled sausage or bacon. Mix together eggs and milk. Pour over meat and hash browns. Top with grated cheddar cheese. Best if prepared the night before and refrigerated. Cook at 350° for 45 minutes to 1 hour.

DAILY TO DO LIST:

GIFT-GIVING BUDGET:

Sunday: _____

_____

_____

Monday: _____

_____

_____

Tuesday: _____

_____

_____

Wednesday: _____

_____

_____

Thursday: _____

_____

_____

Friday: _____

_____

_____

_____

Saturday: _____

_____

_____

CHRISTMAS SHOPPING LIST:

_____

_____

_____

_____

_____

_____

_____

_____

_____

_____

_____

_____

_____

_____

_____

_____

_____

_____

_____

GIFT IDEAS:

_____

_____

_____

_____

_____

_____

_____

_____

_____

_____

_____

_____

DATES TO REMEMBER:

_____

_____

_____

_____

_____

_____

GROUP SESSION

WEEK 3

SAVE YOURSELF FROM HOLIDAY DEBT

Following the arrival activity time, start the group session by reading the introduction page and then open the lesson with prayer.

MAKING A LIST AND CHECKING IT TWICE

Have someone read the scriptures aloud. Encourage the members to plan ahead for the holidays by making a list and setting a budget. I heard it said once that if you fail to plan, then you plan to fail. Planning ahead is key to surviving the holidays!

START SHOPPING NOW

Have someone read the scriptures aloud. Ask the members to share things that stood out in this day's lesson as encouragements for staying on task throughout the holiday season.

WILL THAT BE CASH, CHECK, OR CREDIT?

Have someone read the scriptures aloud. Have the members decide what method of payment they will use this holiday season and discuss the pros and cons of all three methods.

I MADE IT MYSELF!

Have someone read the scriptures aloud. Take time to go over the gift ideas on pages 61- 63, then encourage the members to come up with other creative ideas to share with the group.

FIND A MENTOR

Have someone read the scriptures aloud. Discuss the reasons why it is important to have a mentor. Have someone read page 64 aloud.

Review NOVEMBER WEEK 3 of the Holiday Planning guide.

Conclusion.

WEEK 4

OVERCOMING HOLIDAY SOCIAL ANXIETY

The holiday season is just around the corner and with it comes celebration. It is the time of year when we gather with our family to celebrate the blessings that God has provided for our nation, family, and friends. Thanksgiving is filled with fun, food, and family. Before long the parties, dinners, and gatherings will begin in celebration of Christmas.

It's the most wonderful time of the year! Right? Just as it says in the old Christmas song,

> *There'll be parties for toasting, marshmallows for roasting and caroling out in the snow. There'll be sweet mistletoing and folks telling stories of Christmases long, long ago. So be of good cheer. It's the most wonderful time of the year!*

For some people this is a very difficult time of the year. They become anxious and feelings of doubt and fear overtake them as they think of all the social expectations that lie before them.

In this fourth week of study, we will look at ways to combat the feelings of anxiety and discover creative ways to overcome holiday social anxiety. If you or someone you know experiences HSA (holiday social anxiety), you are not alone.

Anticipate all God wants to teach you this week! Ask Him to show you the things He wants you to see every day as you study His word. Be open to a fresh new approach to life!

DAY 1
The Key to My
Success Is to
Plan Ahead

DAY 2
15 Minutes
Can Make a
Difference

DAY 3
Float Like a
Butterfly

DAY 4
You Have a
Choice

DAY 5
Showers of
Kindness

DAY 1

THE KEY TO MY SUCCESS IS TO PLAN AHEAD

There are so many events that take place during the holidays. There are potluck dinners, teas, parties, holiday shows, gift exchanges, children's programs at church and school, and the list could go on and on. When will we ever find time to buy the gifts, cook the food, buy the tickets, and buy festive attire to wear for the company parties? One can become anxious and overwhelmed just thinking of all that needs to be done in order to "have fun." There is so much to do, and having a plan in place for each event will help alleviate some of the pressures that cause anxiety.

In the space below, list the holiday events that you should attend this year.

_____

_____

_____

Take a moment to look over your list. In the space below, write down the types of people who will be at each event.

_____

_____

_____

Sometimes the fear of the unknown will cause us to experience anxiety. We begin to think about the people who will be at the event and convince ourselves that we will not fit in with the group. We wonder what we could talk about that would be of any interest. Planning ahead allows you to come up with topics of interest. I suggest that you do some homework ahead of time and research general topics to discuss with people by reading the newspapers. Pick up the current issue of a magazine, or look up topics of interest on the Internet. Will you be going to a dinner party at a fancy restaurant? If so, then find out what their signature dishes are so that you can make recommendations to others.

For most people, another topic of interest will be their spouse, boyfriend, or children. Before you leave for the festivities, try and remember the names of those who are special in the lives of your co-workers.

If you have difficulty entering a room alone, make arrangements ahead of time to go to the festivities with another person, or ask them to meet you there so that you may walk in together. According to Bernardo J. Carducci, Ph.D., a professor of psychology and director of the Shyness Research Institute at Indiana University Southeast in New Albany, Indiana, 40% of us are shy. Chances are that someone you know is feeling the same anxiety about the upcoming events as you.

DAY 2

15 MINUTES CAN MAKE A DIFFERENCE

VERSES FOR THE DAY
Oh, the joys of those who do not follow the advice of the wicked, or stand around with sinners, or join in with mockers. But they delight in the law of the Lord, meditating on it day and night. They are like trees planted along the riverbank, bearing fruit each season. Their leaves never wither, and they prosper in all they do. But not the wicked! They are like worthless chaff, scattered by the wind. They will be condemned at the time of judgment. Sinners will have no place among the godly. For the Lord watches over the path of the godly, but the path of the wicked leads to destruction.
Psalm 1

To be "fashionably late" is a thing of the past! I'm not really sure why or how being late ever became socially acceptable, but in this fast-paced environment that we live in today people are beginning to frown on those who arrive late. In an effort to overcome holiday social anxiety, it is important to arrive early. Fifteen minutes early or fifteen minutes late can make the difference on how things go for you at the festivities.

15 MINUTES LATE	15 MINUTES EARLY
Conversations will have already started, making it difficult to join in.	Getting there before the crowd allows you to meet people one-on-one and invite others to join in.
Seats will be chosen and you may end up sitting alone.	Early arrival allows you to pick a table and invite others to sit with you.
No time to offer assistance for the hostess.	Arriving early enables you to help the hostess with the final preparations and to participate in a leading role for the evening.

Recently, I overheard a conversation among three men who were talking about a man who left a legacy in their hometown. He emphasized the importance of arriving on time and taught them that if they weren't fifteen minutes early then they were considered late. This is a good rule to implement in our own lives. For those who experience social anxiety, I would like to suggest that you try arriving early instead of late. It could make a big difference in your overall attitude during the holidays. You might even overcome the dreaded holiday social anxiety.

It is my prayer that you will realize that parties, dinners, and holiday festivities can be fun for you. May you walk into the room of every event this holiday season with God-confidence, remembering that you are never alone...God is always with you!

In the space below, write a prayer to God asking Him to give you the courage needed to arrive early and to approach the festivities with God-confidence.

_____

_____

_____

DAY 3
FLOAT LIKE A BUTTERFLY

"Do not judge others, and you will not be judged. For you will be treated as you treat others. The standard you use in judging is the standard by which you will be judged. And why worry about a speck in your friend's eye when you have a log in your own? How can you think of saying to your friend, 'Let me help you get rid of that speck in your eye,' when you can't see past the log in your own eye?"
Matthew 7:1-4

Then Jesus said, "Come to me, all of you who are weary and carry heavy burdens, and I will give you rest. Take my yoke upon you. Let me teach you, because I am humble and gentle at heart, and you will find rest for your souls. For my yoke is easy to bear, and the burden I give you is light."
Matthew 11:28-30

"For God loved the world so much that he gave his one and only Son, so that everyone who believes in him will not perish but have eternal life. God sent his Son into the world not to judge the world, but to save the world through him."
John 3:16-17

Jesus spoke to the people once more and said, "I am the light of the world. If you follow me, you won't have to walk in darkness, because you will have the light that leads to life."
John 8:12

Have you ever watched a butterfly in the spring? When they transform from the cocoon to the beautiful butterfly, they have a whole new world to explore. They move from one place to another as if to say, "I have missed so much by staying in one place for so long; I feel the need to circulate among the flowers and trees!" They will land on a flower for a short time, and then off they go to the next grouping of flowers or trees. My daughter is a photographer, and once when she was taking photos of my granddaughter, a butterfly landed on her shoulder. It stayed long enough for my daughter to take several shots of my granddaughter and the butterfly together, and then it flew away. Have you ever tried to catch a butterfly? They are so beautiful, and they have a way of brightening a person's day when they appear. They don't stay around very long, and when they leave we wish they would stay. They don't come on too strong. They simply appear graciously and seem to know when the time is right to move on.

In my humble opinion, I believe that some people who experience holiday social anxiety have an inferiority complex. If that is true for you or someone you know, then I want to remind you just how much God loves you. You are very special in His eyes. He even says in the Bible that you are "the apple of his eye."

In the space below, write the words found in John 3:16-17.

_____

_____

_____

Remember that you are not the only person at the social gathering who is feeling shy. Others may be experiencing the same uncomfortable feelings as you. Rather than sticking to one person and one topic all night, talk to a variety of people for brief periods. When others see that you are comfortable talking to lots of people, they will want to approach you.

You just might be amazed at the things you will learn from others if you simply step away from the wall or unglue yourself from the chair, and float like a butterfly!

Enjoy the party!!

DAY 4
YOU HAVE A CHOICE

Let all that I am praise the Lord; with my whole heart, I will praise his holy name. Let all that I am praise the Lord; may I never forget the good things he does for me. He forgives all my sins and heals all my diseases. He redeems me from death and crowns me with love and tender mercies. He fills my life with good things. My youth is renewed like the eagle's! The Lord gives righteousness and justice to all who are treated unfairly. He revealed his character to Moses and his deeds to the people of Israel. The Lord is compassionate and merciful, slow to get angry and filled with unfailing love. He will not constantly accuse us, nor remain angry forever. He does not punish us for all our sins; he does not deal harshly with us, as we deserve. For his unfailing love toward those who fear him is as great as the height of the heavens above the earth. He has removed our sins as far from us as the east is from the west. The Lord is like a father to his children, tender and compassionate to those who fear him. For he knows how weak we are; he remembers we are only dust. Our days on earth are like grass; like wildflowers, we bloom and die. The wind blows, and we are gone—as though we had never been here. But the love of the Lord remains forever with those who fear him. His salvation extends to the children's children of those who are faithful to his covenant, of those who obey his commandments! The Lord has made the heavens his throne; from there he rules over everything. Praise the Lord, you angels, you mighty ones who carry out his plans, listening for each of his commands. Yes, praise the Lord, you armies of angels who serve him and do his will! Praise the Lord, everything he has created, everything in all his kingdom. Let all that I am praise the Lord.
Psalm 103

When you are attending a social event that includes people who you would not usually "hang out" with, you may find yourself in situations that are outside your comfort zone. Remember...just because everyone else is doing "it" does not mean you have to do "it." The choice is yours to make. No one else can make the choice for you.

In Week Two, we touched on the fact that pleasing God is more important than pleasing anyone else. When you arrive at the party, don't allow others to pressure you into doing something that you will regret later. Bear in mind that your behavior at the party could cost you the promotion you were counting on or even worse...it could cost you a job.

Before going to the party, say a prayer to God asking Him to give you strength to resist the temptations that will surround you and to help you do things in a way that will please Him.

You may find yourself in any number of scenarios during the holiday season. Decide how you will handle each situation ahead of time and stay focused in the midst of the peer pressure. Each individual has strengths and weaknesses. Be honest with yourself and accept the fact that you have weaknesses that only through God's grace can be controlled.

In the space below, write a prayer to God asking Him to help you make wise choices and to represent Him wherever you may be throughout the holiday season.

_____

_____

_____

_____

Some people think that their shyness can be overcome through alcohol. The truth of the matter is that alcohol slows information to the brain and makes you a less effective conversationalist. There is good advice in God's word concerning alcohol. We are told not to get drunk. There are many good reasons for this. When your judgment is altered through alcohol consumption, you are more likely to say and do things that are in direct opposition to God. How many times have you had someone come up to you the day after a party and apologize for anything that they may have said or done? They don't remember and just hope they didn't make a fool of themselves. If they had made a choice ahead of time not to allow themselves to get out of control, they would not have the worrisome afterthoughts to deal with. We all have a choice to make, and the best time to make the choice is before you arrive at the party, not during the party.

There are other choices that one must make at parties. If you have strong feelings against dancing and the dance floor is the main attraction for the evening, what choice will you make? If you are a vegetarian and all of the courses served contain meat, what choice will you make? If you are on a strict diet and the food is high in calories, what will you do?

I would like to suggest that every choice you make be a choice that is true to yourself and your relationship with God. Make every choice in light of God's word. Ask this question: "If I choose to do this, will God be pleased with me?" If the answer is "no," then be true to God. Another question to ask is this: "If I choose to do this, will I cause someone else to stumble?" If the answer is "yes," then be true to God and simply choose not to do it.

It's not all about me; it's all about Him! It is very easy to become self-centered when attending a social event, so before arriving ask God to help you be God-centered and not self-centered. This will allow you to make difficult choices with God-confidence!

"Just because you can doesn't mean you should!"
- Sue Ann Cordell

DAY 5
SHOWERS OF KINDNESS

Believe it or not, there will be people at the party who are shyer than you! Decide ahead of time that you will help others who may be shyer than you feel comfortable at the party.

Instead of focusing on being the life of the party, simply focus on being nice. When you see someone who appears to be shyer than you, talk to him or her. Offer to get them something to drink or invite them to sit at your table and make space for them.

By being thoughtful to others, you are making it easier for them to be friendly toward you. Instead of allowing the party to control you, you are now in control of the party.

"Do to others whatever you would like them to do to you. This is the essence of all that is taught in the law and the prophets."
Matthew 7:12

Jesus teaches us a simple technique on how to successfully treat others. Try and put yourself in the other person's position at the party. If you are shy, then you have an idea as to how they might be feeling. Treat them the way you wish others would treat you and be nice to those around you.

VERSES FOR THE DAY

People ruin their lives by their own foolishness and then are angry at the Lord.
Proverbs 19:3

Get rid of all bitterness, rage, anger, harsh words, and slander, as well as all types of evil behavior. Instead, be kind to each other, tenderhearted, forgiving one another, just as God through Christ has forgiven you.
Ephesians 4:31-32

For we are God's masterpiece. He has created us anew in Christ Jesus, so we can do the good things he planned for us long ago.
Ephesians 2:10

Live wisely among those who are not believers, and make the most of every opportunity.
Colossians 4:5

Now may the Lord of peace himself give you his peace at all times and in every situation. The Lord be with you all.
2 Thessalonians 3:16

Sometimes shy people appear to be snobs. They seem to be unhappy and act as if they just want to be left alone. Before arriving at the party, put on your "party face." Smiles are contagious, and even if you really are unhappy about being there and you prefer to be left alone, try to look happy and show kindness to others. The evening will move along quicker that way, and by being thoughtful to others you may gain a new friend.

Another area of kindness that is often overlooked is toward those who put the party together. There is a lot of work involved in planning a holiday party. Take time to thank those who provided this for you. You might not agree with everything that is done, but the efforts were made on behalf of all employees, friends, or members of the organization.

As you attend the social events of the holidays, look at people through God's eyes and remember that He loves us all. Treat everyone with kindness; that within itself is a gift you can give to others!

In the space below, write a prayer to God asking Him to show you the people who need the gift of kindness at the parties you will attend during the holiday season.

_____

_____

_____

Make the most of every opportunity. Show kindness to those around you and have the best holiday party season ever!

HOLIDAY PLANNING
NOVEMBER
WEEK 4

TO DO LIST

Christmas Plans:

___ Package and mail gifts.

___ Update gift list.

___ Send out invitations for Christmas parties.

SURVIVOR TIPS

Why not wrap kitchen gifts in a big dish towel and decorate with a scouring pad for the bow. Add a wooden spoon as the tag; use a felt pen to write on the handle "to" and "from."

Use cellophane for those "How am I going to wrap that?" gifts. It works well for baskets, buckets, Christmas plates of goodies, plants, or flowers.

Gift bags are great for a quick, easy, decorative way to wrap. They are reusable too! Line the bag with contrasting tissue paper, or wrap your gift item in tissue. Add a bow to the handle with a gift tag.

Always get a courtesy box, tissue, and ribbon whenever you buy anything at a department store or where the giftwrap is free. Save them in your giftwrap center for the times you need them.

Gift boxes and containers - The decorated ones need only a ribbon! When appropriate, use tins, ceramic containers, flowerpots, buckets, pails, and baskets.

Large silver, black, or green plastic garbage bags may be just the thing to hide a large gift. Add a banner, large bow, and stickers. It will look just like Santa's pack!

Watch your finances carefully!

Plan some time for yourself. You can read a book, listen to music, take a bubble bath by candlelight, get a haircut, have your nails done, or maybe buy yourself a new outfit.

DESSERT PARTY

Christmas Punch
1 quart cranberry juice cocktail, chilled
1 quart apple juice, chilled
1 quart club soda, chilled
1 quart sparkling white grape juice, chilled
Combine all ingredients in punch bowl. Float an ice ring of orange slices
(turned sideways) and cherries.

Ambrosia
12 medium oranges
¼ cup confectioner's sugar
¼ cup orange juice
1 fresh pineapple cut into bite-sized pieces
1 cup flaked coconut
With sharp knife, cut and peel off each orange, cutting deep enough
to remove all white membrane. Cut along both sides of each, dividing
membrane, and lift out sections from center, keeping sections whole. Save
¼ cup juice. In large bowl combine juice with sugar until dissolved. Add
oranges, pineapple, and coconut, reserving 1 tablespoon coconut for garnish.
Toss lightly. Can be prepared in advance to this point. Cover and refrigerate
up to 24 hours. Sprinkle reserved coconut on top.

Iced Almonds
2 cups whole blanched almonds
1 cup sugar
4 tablespoons butter
1 teaspoon vanilla
salt
Heat almonds in heavy skillet along with sugar and butter. Stir until almonds
are toasted and sugar is brown—about 15 minutes. Stir in vanilla. Drop in
clusters. Sprinkle with a little salt. Cool.

Chocolate Balls
1 cup butter
1 ½ cups graham cracker crumbs
½ cup chopped pecans
1 cup coconut
1 pound box confectioners' sugar
1 tablespoon vanilla
1 jar (12 ounces) crunchy peanut butter
1 package (6 ounces) semi-sweet chocolate chips
⅛ pound paraffin

Over medium heat, melt butter in large container; stir in graham cracker crumbs, pecans, coconut, confectioner's sugar, and vanilla. Add peanut butter and mix well. Shape into 1-inch balls and lay on wax paper. Chill for 1 hour. In the top of the double boiler, melt chocolate and paraffin together. Using a long toothpick, dip each ball into melted chocolate and return to wax paper. When finished, cover hole made by toothpick with a few drops of melted chocolate. Allow to cool before storing in air-tight container. (makes 8 dozen)

Individual Cheese Cakes
2 packages (8 ounces each) of cream cheese
3 eggs, separated
¾ cup sugar
butter to grease pan
¾ cup graham cracker crumbs
½ cup sour cream
1 ½ teaspoon sugar
½ teaspoon vanilla flavoring

Beat together cream cheese, egg yolks, and sugar until light and fluffy. Beat egg whites until soft peaks form and fold into cheese mixture. Butter small muffin pans generously. Put one rounded teaspoon of graham cracker crumbs in each buttered muffin cup and shake until sides and bottoms are well coated. Empty out excess crumbs and reuse. Fill each cup almost full with cream cheese mixture. Bake in a preheated 350° oven for 15-20 minutes. Remove from pans and cool. Combine sour cream, 1 ½ tablespoons sugar, and vanilla. Fill indented places with ½ teaspoon topping when ready to serve.
(makes 48 small cakes)

Mother's Divinity

½ cup light corn syrup
2 cups sugar
½ cup cold water
1 teaspoon vanilla
2 egg whites

Mix together all ingredients except egg whites. Cook in a heavy saucepan over medium heat. Stir until all sugar dissolves. Stir constantly until mixture comes to a boil. Reduce heat and cook without stirring until mixture reaches 250° (firm ball) on candy thermometer. Beat egg whites until stiff. Pour ½ mixture over egg whites while beating with electric mixer. Cook remaining mixture to 272° (soft crack). Pour this mixture into the first (containing egg whites) a little at a time while still beating with mixer. Drop by teaspoon onto wax paper. (makes 4 dozen)

Along with Christmas punch, serve coffee and a variety of hot teas.

DAILY TO DO LIST:

Sunday: _____

_____

_____

Monday: _____

_____

_____

Tuesday: _____

_____

_____

Wednesday: _____

_____

_____

Thursday: _____

_____

_____

Friday: _____

_____

_____

_____

Saturday: _____

_____

_____

GIFT-GIVING BUDGET:

_____

_____

_____

_____

_____

_____

_____

_____

_____

_____

_____

_____

_____

_____

_____

_____

_____

_____

_____

_____

_____

_____

_____

_____

_____

_____

CHRISTMAS SHOPPING LIST:

_____

_____

_____

_____

_____

_____

_____

_____

_____

_____

_____

_____

_____

_____

_____

_____

_____

_____

_____

_____

GIFT IDEAS:

_____

_____

_____

_____

_____

_____

_____

_____

_____

_____

_____

_____

_____

_____

GIFTS TO BE MAILED:

_____

_____

_____

_____

_____

_____

GROUP SESSION

OVERCOMING HOLIDAY SOCIAL ANXIETY

Following the arrival activity time, start the group session by reading the introduction page and then open the lesson with prayer.

THE KEY TO MY SUCCESS IS TO PLAN AHEAD

Have someone read the scriptures aloud. Ask the group to share their answers to the questions on page 72. Ask them to share the highlights of this lesson with others in the group. What helpful hints did they pick up that will enable them to overcome some of their inhibitions this year?

15 MINUTES CAN MAKE A DIFFERENCE

Have someone read Psalm 1 aloud. Talk about the importance of arriving early and the reasons why this is critical for those wishing to overcome the fear of the crowd. Discuss what it means to have God-confidence.

FLOAT LIKE A BUTTERFLY

Have someone read the scriptures aloud. Discuss the beauty of the butterfly. Think of ways to be more like the social butterfly and less like the slug who is stuck to the wall! Encourage everyone to go into the room with a plan and to truly enjoy the party this year!

YOU HAVE A CHOICE

Have the group read the scripture aloud together. Planning ahead is the key to making "right choices." Have someone read pages 79 and 80 and open the floor up for discussion. Have the group read the quote at the top of page 80 aloud together.

SHOWERS OF KINDNESS

Have someone read the scriptures aloud. Encourage the members to pay attention to the needs of others at the parties they attend. Discuss the things that stood out in this lesson.

Review NOVEMBER WEEK 4 of the Holiday Planning guide.

Conclusion.

WEEK 5

CREATING MEMORIES

If you were to ask your family members to share their favorite holiday memory, you may be surprised how few meals and toys they mention. This question was asked at a church Christmas party one year, and very few could recall special holiday memories. If this is the case for your family, then it's time to create lasting memories. Toys get broken, but a memory lasts forever.

In this fifth week of study, we will brainstorm about ways to create memories for others. We will also look into God's word daily for encouragement, direction, and wisdom.

DAY 1
It's a Family
Tradition

Anticipate all that God wants to teach you this week! Ask Him to show you the things He wants you to see every day as you study His word. Be open to a fresh new approach to life!

DAY 2
Things Worth
Repeating

DAY 3
Kids in the
Kitchen

DAY 4
What's in Your
Attic?

DAY 5
Sentimental
Journal

DAY 1

IT'S A FAMILY TRADITION

What does the phrase "It's a Family Tradition" mean to you? Does your family have certain ways that they celebrate special occasions? Do you go to the same restaurant every year for Christmas Eve? Is there a special food item that is served on Christmas Day? Do your children leave milk and cookies for Santa, and an apple for Rudolph?

In the space below, list the family traditions that come to mind when thinking about the holidays.

_____

_____

_____

_____

_____

_____

VERSES FOR THE DAY

Mary responded, "Oh, how my soul praises the Lord. How my spirit rejoices in God my Savior! For he took notice of his lowly servant girl, and from now on all generations will call me blessed. For the Mighty One is holy, and he has done great things for me. He shows mercy from generation to generation to all who fear him. His mighty arm has done tremendous things! He has scattered the proud and haughty ones. He has brought down princes from their thrones and exalted the humble. He has filled the hungry with good things and sent the rich away with empty hands. He has helped his servant Israel and remembered to be merciful. For he made this promise to our ancestors, to Abraham and his children forever." Luke 1:46-55

Shout with joy to the Lord, all the earth! Worship the Lord with gladness. Come before him, singing with joy. Acknowledge that the Lord is God! He made us, and we are his. We are his people, the sheep of his pasture. Enter his gates with thanksgiving; go into his courts with praise. Give thanks to him and praise his name. For the Lord is good. His unfailing love continues forever, and his faithfulness continues to each generation. Psalm 100

We live in an unstable society. The average tenure for employment with a corporation is three to five years. Men and women are changing jobs and locations more than they did in the past. Divorces still occur at a very high rate. Latchkey children are considered to be the "norm" in most households. Because of this instability, we need to establish family traditions more now than ever before.

When forming your family traditions, remember what really matters. Family should come first. As you begin to set your family traditions, it is good to carry on some of the traditions from your own childhood. Just remember that you are a grownup now and your children need to have good memories of times at your home, not always at Grandma's.

Even though I am an only child, my parents always made sure that I was home on Christmas morning. I remember how excited and nervous I would be when I woke up on that very special morning each year. Santa always left my gifts, unwrapped, under the tree. Since he got milk and cookies most everywhere he went on Christmas Eve, I left him a bologna sandwich with extra mayonnaise, and every year the same thing happened...he ate the whole sandwich! It wasn't until I was eight years old that I discovered that Santa and Dad both enjoyed the same kind of sandwich. How coincidental was that? Once all of the gifts were opened, we enjoyed a delicious breakfast together as a family, and then off we went to spend the day with other family members. Sometimes we would travel to Johnson City, Tennessee, and other times we would travel to Jacksonville, Florida.

When I grew up and married, my husband and I began to form our own traditions. They were much like the ones we had experienced with our parents. Now that our children are grown, they too are carrying on family traditions with their children.

It's fun to have set rituals throughout the holidays! The weekend following Thanksgiving is the traditional time for us to decorate for Christmas. The tree goes up, the outside lights are strung, the classic Christmas movies are dusted off, and we begin to watch them and reminisce about the days gone by. I also have a basket full of Christmas books for children that I place by the fireplace. I enjoy reading the Little Golden Books and when my adult children stop by, they will pick up a book and begin to read and reminisce too. I have a reindeer that sings *Grandma Got Run Over By a Reindeer* and a Christmas tree that sings *We Wish You a Merry Christmas*. Several years ago, I purchased a musical clock, and every hour on the hour it plays a different Christmas carol. Children love this clock, and every year they look forward to hearing the music that plays very loudly every hour on the hour. I think my husband would prefer that I not bring this clock out each year, but it has become a family tradition for me to do so.

Children are so cute, and I have so many wonderful memories of my children that I will cherish for a lifetime! When my son was three years old, he wanted to sing his favorite Christmas carol. I asked him what it was and he said, "Si-lee-int Night, Ho-lee-int, Night." To this day, when I hear "Silent Night" played or sung, I smile and my mind drifts back to those years when my cute little red-haired boy would walk around the house singing his version of his favorite Christmas carol. I remember when my daughter was an angel in the children's Christmas program at church. She got to wear angel wings, and the whole time she was standing on the stage she was moving her shoulders from side to side so that her wings would move like she thought a "real angel's" wings would do.

Our whole family attends a Christmas Eve candlelight service each year. We sit together and partake of the Lord's Supper as a family. This is a tradition that I cherish. It reminds us once again of the things that really matter. Following the candlelight service, we invite close friends to stop by our house for some light refreshments. Our children usually stick around after everyone else leaves because they still like to open one gift from Mom and Dad on Christmas Eve. Then everyone goes home and our house is quiet until 8:00 the next morning. Our children and their children come back to our house for the traditional gift exchange and breakfast. What great memories!

Traditions are established by repeating the same things year after year. As you go through this holiday season, make notes of the events that are worth repeating next year. Before you know it, you will have family traditions, and your legacy will be carried on from generation to generation.

"The great value of traditions comes as they give a family a sense of identity, a belongingness." - Dr. James Dobson

DAY 2
THINGS WORTH REPEATING

VERSES FOR THE DAY

At that time there was a man in Jerusalem named Simeon. He was righteous and devout and was eagerly waiting for the Messiah to come and rescue Israel. The Holy Spirit was upon him and had revealed to him that he would not die until he had seen the Lord's Messiah. That day the Spirit led him to the Temple. So when Mary and Joseph came to present the baby Jesus to the Lord as the law required, Simeon was there. He took the child in his arms and praised God, saying, "Sovereign Lord, now let your servant die in peace, as you have promised. I have seen your salvation, which you have prepared for all people. He is a light to reveal God to the nations, and he is the glory of your people Israel!" Jesus' parents were amazed at what was being said about him. Then Simeon blessed them, and he said to Mary, the baby's mother, "This child is destined to cause many in Israel to fall, but he will be a joy to many others. He has been sent as a sign from God, but many will oppose him. As a result, the deepest thoughts of many hearts will be revealed. And a sword will pierce your very soul."
Luke 2:25-35

Teaching about Giving to the Needy

"Watch out! Don't do your good deeds publicly, to be admired by others, for you will lose the reward from your Father in heaven. When you give to someone in need, don't do as the hypocrites do—blowing trumpets in the synagogues and streets to call attention to their acts of charity! I tell you the truth, they have received all the reward they will ever get. But when you give to someone in need, don't let your left hand know what your right hand is doing. Give your gifts in private, and your Father, who sees everything, will reward you."
Matthew 6:1-4

When my grandmother would prepare a special meal for guests or family, she had a bowl that she would use for the occasion. It was a clear glass bowl with four legs and a beveled design embossed into it. When she passed away, I inherited the bowl. When I prepare a special meal for guests or family, I make sure that I use the same bowl. This bowl is very special to me because it brings back wonderful memories of my grandmother. My children did not have the privilege of knowing anything about her, but when I pass away, I venture to say that one of my children will probably prepare special meals for guests or family and use the same bowl. Even simple things such as this are worth repeating. I have seen replicas of this bowl in antique shops. I'm sure it was an inexpensive bowl when my grandmother purchased it, but through the years it has become priceless to me.

When I was in the fourth grade my Sunday School teacher required all of her students to memorize Luke 2:1–20. This is the story of Jesus' birth. We started working on the memorization in October and were expected to recite it in front of the whole class on the first Sunday in December. Even now, when I hear the words from this scripture text, I can picture Mrs. Styons standing over me as I worked so diligently on my assignment. The Bible is a powerful tool in our fight against temptation, depression, discouragement, and all types of sin. Memorizing that scripture taught me the importance of having God's word in my heart at all times. I still memorize scripture and encourage others to do the same. Thank you, Mrs. Styons! The things you taught me are worth repeating!

Each year during the holiday season, we pick ornaments off of the "Angel Tree" at church. On each ornament are items that families in need would like to have for Christmas. I close my eyes and pray as I pick four ornaments from the tree. Then when I am shopping for the items requested, I say another prayer for the individual who will receive the gift. I pray that they will realize how much God loves them and because of his love, their needs will be met. I look forward to the "Angel Tree" project each year, and it is worth repeating again and again!

In the space below, list things that are important to you. List things that you feel are worth repeating this year.

_____

_____

_____

Laughter is good for the soul! For many people the classic Christmas movies are worth repeating. Have you ever talked to a man or woman about the famous movie entitled *A Christmas Story*? Have you noticed that they always have a smile on their face as they describe their favorite scenes from the movie? *It's a Wonderful Life, Charlie Brown's Christmas, Rudolph, the Red-nosed Reindeer, Frosty the Snowman, Christmas Vacation, A Christmas Carol, The Night the Animals Talked, How the Grinch Stole Christmas, Home Alone, Earnest Saves Christmas*...these are a few of the movies that are worth repeating.

Times spent with friends and family members alike are things worth repeating.

Too many times we get caught up in the hustle and bustle of the holiday season and don't really savor the traditions. I value the times spent with family and friends who have gone on to be with the Lord. No one is promised a tomorrow. The folks who are with you today may not be around next year. Enjoy every moment that you have together!

Things done for others during the holiday season are worth repeating!

DAY 3

KIDS IN THE KITCHEN

Remember the old commercial for "Shake and Bake"? A little girl stands in the kitchen with her mother and with pride, she displays an appetizing platter of chicken and says, with a southern accent, "It's Shake and Bake and I helped!" Children love to help in the kitchen. There was a time when dishwashers were not as common as they are today, and some of my fondest memories with my mother were times when we shared the dishwashing duties...she would wash and I would dry. During that time, we would solve the problems of the world or sing, laugh, and dream big dreams together.

I love to host tea parties and have enjoyed teaching my granddaughters all about tea etiquette. When they spend the night at my house, we have tea parties. We make cream cheese sandwiches and use cookie cutters to shape them into stars, hearts, or flowers. Then we place the sandwiches on one side of a fancy plate. On the other side, we place fancy cookies or chocolate truffles. We will cover a small table with a pretty towel or tablecloth and then heat our water for the tea. I have many teacups and saucers, and we choose our favorite for the day and place a tea bag in the cups. This allows the tea to steep while we finish preparing for the party. A tea party is not complete without a hat, so we go to Nana's closet and find hats to wear. Once we have everything in place for our party,

VERSES FOR THE DAY

O God, you have taught me from my earliest childhood, and I constantly tell others about the wonderful things you do. Now that I am old and gray, do not abandon me, O God. Let me proclaim your power to this new generation, your mighty miracles to all who come after me.
Psalm 71:17-18

Direct your children onto the right path, and when they are older, they will not leave it.
Proverbs 22:6

One day some parents brought their children to Jesus so he could lay his hands on them and pray for them. But the disciples scolded the parents for bothering him. But Jesus said, "Let the children come to me.

Don't stop them! For the Kingdom of Heaven belongs to those who are like these children." And he placed his hands on their heads and blessed them before he left.
Matthew 19:13-15

Anna, a prophet, was also there in the Temple. She was the daughter of Phanuel from the tribe of Asher, and she was very old. Her husband died when they had been married only seven years. Then she lived as a widow to the age of eighty-four. She never left the Temple but stayed there day and night, worshiping God with fasting and prayer. She came along just as Simeon was talking with Mary and Joseph, and she began praising God. She talked about the child

to everyone who had been waiting expectantly for God to rescue Jerusalem. When Jesus' parents had fulfilled all the requirements of the law of the Lord, they returned home to Nazareth in Galilee. There the child grew up healthy and strong. He was filled with wisdom, and God's favor was on him.
Luke 2:36-40

we play soft music and enjoy "girl talk" while sipping on our tea and enjoying our fancy foods. When the party is over, we clean up together and talk about our plans for the next tea party. I cherish these times! Do we make a mess in the kitchen? Oh yes! Having kids in the kitchen can be challenging at times, but the lessons that they learn are valuable. Actually, I have learned many valuable lessons from them too!

The kitchen should be considered a happy place for people to congregate. Do you have a welcoming kitchen? Some of life's greatest lessons are learned in the kitchen. I have a special drawer in my kitchen just for the grandkids. They learn early on that they can open this particular drawer and always find special treats just for them. They also learn early on that they are not allowed to open the other drawers because of the sharp objects that may harm them. Sometimes they find small cars in the drawer. Other times they find marshmallows, cereal, cookies, snack bars, or candy. Now that they are getting older, they will usually get something out of their drawer and climb onto a bar stool and talk to me as I finish preparing the food. As they get older, I feel certain we will have some deep conversations in the kitchen. I look forward to having kids in the kitchen for many years to come!

My children are grown now, and we still find ourselves in the kitchen when we have something of importance to talk about. As you create memories for your friends and family, create a kid-friendly environment for your children, grandchildren, nieces, and nephews. The memories will last a lifetime!

RECIPE FOR SUCCESS
We pray for children
> Who sneak Popsicles before supper,
> Who erase holes in math workbooks,
> Who can never find their shoes.

And we pray for those
> Who stare at photographers from behind barbed wire,
> Who can't bound down the street in a new pair of sneakers,
> Who never "counted potatoes,"
> Who are born in places we wouldn't be caught dead in,
> Who never go to the circus,
> Who live in an X-rated world.

We pray for children
> Who bring us sticky kisses and fistfuls of dandelions,
> Who hug us in a hurry and forget their lunch money.

And we pray for those
> Who never get dessert,
> Who have no safe blanket to drag behind them,
> Who watch their parents watch them die,

Who can't find any bread to steal,

Who don't have any rooms to clean up,

Whose pictures aren't on anybody's dresser,

Whose monsters are real.

We pray for children

Who spend all their allowance before Tuesday,

Who throw tantrums in the grocery store and pick at their food,

Who like ghost stories,

Who shove dirty clothes under the bed and never rinse out the tub,

Who get visits from the tooth fairy,

Who don't like to be kissed in front of the carpool,

Who squirm in church and scream in the phone,

Whose tears we sometimes laugh at and whose smiles can make us cry.

And we pray for those

Whose nightmares come in the daytime,

Who will eat anything,

Who have never seen a dentist,

Who aren't spoiled by anybody,

Who go to bed hungry and cry themselves to sleep,

Who live and move, but have no being.

We pray for children who want to be carried,

For those we never give up on and for those who don't get a second chance.

For those we smother...and for those who will grab the hand of anybody kind enough to offer it.

Please offer your hand to them so that no child is left behind because we did not act.

- Marion Wright Edelman, *The Measure of Our Success: A Letter to My Children and Yours*

DAY 4
WHAT'S IN YOUR ATTIC?

VERSES FOR THE DAY

Then Jesus returned to Galilee, filled with the Holy Spirit's power. Reports about him spread quickly through the whole region. He taught regularly in their synagogues and was praised by everyone.
When he came to the village of Nazareth, his boyhood home, he went as usual to the synagogue on the Sabbath and stood up to read the Scriptures. The scroll of Isaiah the prophet was handed to him. He unrolled the scroll and found the place where this was written: "The Spirit of the Lord is upon me, for he has anointed me to bring Good News to the poor. He has sent me to proclaim that captives will be released, that the blind will see, that the oppressed will be set free, and that the time of the Lord's favor has come." He rolled up the scroll, handed it back to the attendant, and sat down. All eyes in the synagogue looked at him intently. Then he began to speak to them. "The Scripture you've just heard has been fulfilled this very day!"
Luke 4:14-21

I have hidden your word in my heart, that I might not sin against you.
Psalm 119:11

I would love to tell you that I have every paper and every craft that my children made when they were in school, but I can't honestly say that I kept everything. I did, however, keep all of their report cards, sentimental poems, class pictures, yearbooks, and school pictures. I kept their handprints, newspaper clippings, trophies, and awards. Ever so often, I think maybe I should toss some of this stuff, but then as I go back through the items, I just can't bear to part with it!

Now that I have grandchildren, I am collecting some of the same items about them. I have come to realize that's what attics are for! I not only have items from my children and their children, but I have keepsakes from my childhood, my mother's childhood, and my grandmother's childhood. I know it sounds like I must have lots of things, but really the things that mean the most to me fit into three boxes. My attic has just enough space to hold things such as these.

I knew that I was an important part of my grandmother's life, but I didn't realize how much until after her death. She kept all of my papers, letters, newspaper clippings, and pictures in suitcases. I love to open the suitcases and browse through those old papers!

It's like going back in time. It reminds me of times when she and I laughed together and cried together. There are pictures of my father when he was a child and pictures of my grandmother as a child. My Christian heritage dates back to the 1800s, and if it weren't for the things in my attic, I might not have been aware of this information.

Pictures really are worth a thousand words! Do you have pictures of your family neatly tucked away for generations that will come after you? When I was ten years old, I decided to "help" my mother with some of our photo albums. There were old pictures that seemed to fall out of the albums whenever we would try and look at them. So I decided to take scotch tape and tape horizontally across each picture. Needless to say those pictures are ruined. It's a good idea to find a safe place to keep your family treasures. Have you considered scrapbooking? It has become a popular pastime for many these days. This is a way to capture the photographic moment for others to enjoy for many years to come!

My husband was a football player in high school. My son played football in high school and in college. Every year they "lettered" in the sport and received a "letter jacket." I keep those in my cedar chest. When Bobby was little, his grandfather used to buy him Army jackets and sew real Army patches on them. Now that my son has a little boy, he is wearing his Daddy's jackets. If I had not saved them, Rowan would have missed out on that memory. My guess is that these jackets will be worn by the next generation too. These things may not mean anything to you at the time, but before getting rid of them, ask yourself if other family members might have an interest in the years to come.

My mother-in-law found a dress in her mother's attic that belonged to her when she was 3 years old. She passed it on to me for my daughter to wear when she was three. This was a special dress, and it is now back in the attic for another little girl in the family to wear sometime.

When my daughter got married, she used my wedding Bible as part of her bouquet. What's in your attic? Creating memories for others can be as simple as pulling out things from the past that you have saved through the years.

My grandsons are now playing with cars and action figures that my son enjoyed when he was little. Each time my son sees the toys from the past, he has a story to pass along and a memory that warms our hearts all over again.

In the space below, write about a memory from your family that is tucked away in the attic.

_____

_____

_____

We are creating memories for those around us every day. In the space below, write a prayer to God thanking Him for the good memories from your past.

_____

_____

_____

Some of the memories from our past may not be pleasant ones. Thank God for the good memories and ask Him to help you learn from the unpleasant ones. As you go through the days, months, and years ahead, do your best to create good memories for those around you.

May God bless you and your family with happy memories and fun treasures to put in your attic for generations that will come after you!

DAY 5
SENTIMENTAL JOURNAL

One of the best words of advice given to me was to put every event in writing. Journal about your life so that you can look back on all God has done for you personally through the years. When I first started writing in a journal, I wasn't sure just what to write, and over the course of time I have learned that it doesn't really matter what I write because there are no strict rules to follow.

A journal can be used for many things: to record history, to keep track of the weather, to outline one's work, to gather raw materials for writing and speaking. Today, I want to introduce you to journaling at its deepest level...for spiritual growth.

A spiritual journal is a book in which you keep a personal record of events in your life, or your different relationships, your feelings, and your greatest adventures. You will discover more about yourself when you keep a journal.

Barbara Johnson describes a spiritual journal like this: "As a new way for you to add joy to your life. When good things happen to lighten your load and brighten your day, write them down." When someone pays you a compliment, write it down. When you remember nice things from the past, write them down. Let the journal become a personal treasure chest—your collected thoughts of hope, gladness, and love. She says, "If you find yourself slipping into the clutches of drudgery, pessimism, and gloom, your journal can help you stay in a frame of mind that celebrates life instead of letting it simply go by or become bogged down in the miseries. It will help you develop a sense of humor. It will bring a smile to your face and hope to your heart. It will be a treasury of gladness to inspire for years to come."

VERSES FOR THE DAY

The Lord is my shepherd; I have all that I need. He lets me rest in green meadows; he leads me beside peaceful streams. He renews my strength. He guides me along right paths, bringing honor to his name. Even when I walk through the darkest valley, I will not be afraid, for you are close beside me. Your rod and your staff protect and comfort me. You prepare a feast for me in the presence of my enemies. You honor me by anointing my head with oil. My cup overflows with blessings. Surely your goodness and unfailing love will pursue me all the days of my life, and I will live in the house of the Lord forever. Psalm 23

For me personally, I like to simply describe my journals this way: My journals are records of my personal spiritual journey. They take me into the very presence of God and show me how my faith and His grace and mercy have brought me to where I am today.

To begin, you just need a notebook, pen, and Bible. Think about your day and ask yourself the following questions.

1. As I look back on the day, what were the most significant events?

_____

_____

2. In what ways was this day unique, different from other days?

_____

_____

3. Did I have any particularly significant conversations?

_____

_____

4. How did I feel during the day? What were the emotional high points or low points? Why did I feel as I did? Is God trying to tell me anything through these feelings?

_____

_____

5. Did I find myself worrying about anything today? Can I turn that worry into a prayer?

_____

_____

As you begin to journal, don't take it too seriously. It should not be looked at as a grim chore. Let your journal be a time for you, an enjoyable, quiet time, even a gift you give yourself. Relax and enjoy it!

Your journal can be an aid to your devotional life. Prepare by reading scriptures. Ponder over the events of your day and the blessings that God has given you throughout the day. Pray—Write your prayers in your journal.

If I were asked the question, "If my house were on fire and I could only get a few things out of the house, what would they be?" I would answer without hesitation, "I want my journals – they are the story of my life; they are my legacy for generations who will come after me. They remind me and inspire me to hold on to my faith through the good times and the bad."

I encourage you to try it! My prayer for you is that your relationship with God will grow daily as you enjoy recording in your very own sentimental journal.

The words recorded in the Bible were a result of journaling. David wrote down his thoughts and prayers, and we now have the privilege of learning from him. The apostles who were eyewitnesses of Jesus' life here on earth wrote down the historical events for us to have in this day and age. Journaling is a learning tool for the writer and the reader. Paul was such a great writer and teacher. All of the writings in scripture can be considered journals. I thank God for those men and women who were obedient to God's call and wrote down the events and teachings for each and every one of us.

When will you begin your sentimental journal?

DECEMBER

WEEK 5

SURVIVOR TIPS

As a family, decide to incorporate one new tradition into your holiday season this year.

Invite someone who is alone to celebrate the decorations and festivities, or just a pleasant meal. Elderly people, college students far from home, and singles often miss their families and could use a cheery celebration.

Manger Tradition

Set up a manger scene, homemade from wood or ceramics, or a purchased one. Everything is displayed except the Baby Jesus. Each time a child in the family does a good deed on his own, he gets to put a few pieces of straw in the manger. On Christmas morning, when there is sufficient straw in the manger, Jesus will appear in his bed. Watch the excitement of the children on Christmas morning when they race to see if Baby Jesus is there.

Tree Trimming

Make this a family tradition! Play Christmas music and light a few candles during the evening. Make an easy meal or pull a casserole out of the freezer. Have cookies and hot apple cider ready for "halftime."

Candles add a wonderful mood to Christmas decorating. When candles drip on your pretty tablecloths, don't despair! Lay paper towels on the ironing board over and under the drips and iron the wax spots with a medium-to-hot iron. Keep moving the paper towels until the wax is absorbed into them. Presto! The wax is gone and the cloth is saved.

If you are beginning to feel overwhelmed, do whatever time and finances will allow, but do treat yourself to a hair appointment, manicure, or massage. And try to get plenty of sleep and exercise.

TO DO LIST

Christmas Plans:

___ Decorate for the season.

___ Finish Christmas shopping, update "Gifts-Given" list.

___ Finish holiday baking.

CARAMEL ORANGE RING

2 packages Texas-style biscuits (20)

8 ounces orange marmalade

¾ cup walnut or pecans

1½ sticks margarine or butter

1 tablespoon cinnamon

3 cups brown sugar

Melt margarine. Spray Bundt pan with non-stick spray. In bottom of Bundt pan spread marmalade. Sprinkle with nuts. Roll biscuits in margarine then in brown sugar mixed with cinnamon. Set biscuits on edge around Bundt pan. Bake at 350° for 45 minutes. Wait one minute after baking and turn upside down.

GARLIC CHEDDAR BISCUITS

2 cups Bisquick

²/₃ cup milk

½ cup shredded cheddar cheese

¼ cup butter

¼ teaspoon garlic powder

Mix first three ingredients vigorously for 30 seconds. Drop by spoonfuls onto ungreased cookie sheet. Bake at 350° for 8-10 minutes. Mix butter and garlic powder; brush on hot biscuits.

CRANBERRY PUNCH

4 cups cranberry juice

1½ cups sugar

4 cups pineapple juice

1 tablespoon almond extract

2 quarts ginger ale

Mix all ingredients. Chill or add ice cubes.

(Cranberry/raspberry juice mixed in equal parts with ginger ale, with raspberry sherbet floating on top, tastes delicious, and looks festive when set out in a large crystal punch bowl.)

CREAM CHEESE, CELERY, AND WALNUT SANDWICHES

4 ounces cream cheese, room temperature

¼ celery heart, very finely chopped

¼ cup diced walnuts

white or whole wheat bread, parsley sprigs for garnish

In a small bowl, beat cream cheese until smooth. Mix in celery and walnuts. Make sandwiches with cheese mixture. Trim off crust of bread and cut sandwiches into rectangles or triangles. Garnish with sprigs of parsley.

DAILY TO DO LIST:

Sunday: _____

_____

_____

Monday: _____

_____

_____

Tuesday: _____

_____

_____

Wednesday: _____

_____

_____

Thursday: _____

_____

_____

Friday: _____

_____

_____

Saturday: _____

_____

_____

GIFT-GIVING BUDGET:

_____

_____

_____

_____

_____

_____

_____

_____

_____

_____

_____

_____

_____

_____

_____

_____

_____

_____

_____

_____

_____

_____

_____

_____

CHRISTMAS SHOPPING LIST:

_____

_____

_____

_____

_____

_____

_____

_____

_____

_____

_____

_____

_____

_____

_____

_____

_____

_____

_____

_____

_____

_____

_____

GIFTS-GIVEN LIST:

_____

_____

_____

_____

_____

_____

_____

_____

_____

_____

_____

_____

_____

_____

GIFTS RECEIVED:

_____

_____

_____

_____

_____

_____

_____

GROUP SESSION
WEEK 5

CREATING MEMORIES

Following the arrival activity time, start the group session by reading the
introduction page and then open the lesson with prayer.

IT'S A FAMILY TRADITION

Have someone read the scriptures aloud. Allow time for the members to share
their traditions with each other. Encourage them to start at least one new
tradition for their family this holiday season.

THINGS WORTH REPEATING

Have someone read the scriptures aloud. In the same way that they shared
their traditions, encourage the members to brainstorm about ways they can
carry on traditions for generations to come.

KIDS IN THE KITCHEN

Have someone read the scriptures aloud. Ask the members to tell a funny story
or a sentimental story about a time they were in the kitchen with a child.
Read aloud "Recipe for Success" on pages 98 and 99.

WHAT'S IN YOUR ATTIC?

Have someone read the scriptures aloud. Encourage the members to share
their answers to the questions on pages 101 and 102.

SENTIMENTAL JOURNAL

Have someone read the scripture aloud. Ask the members to share their
answers to the questions on page 104. Encourage the members to start
journaling. Set an example by starting a journal of your own. I promise, you will
be glad you did!

Review DECEMBER WEEK 5 of the Holiday Planning guide.

Conclusion.

WEEK 6

THE REASON FOR THE SEASON

We are in the midst of the holiday season. The department stores are crowded, the Salvation Army is ringing bells in front of stores, Christmas decorations are lining the streets and houses, and children are filled with excitement as they stand in line to talk to Santa Claus. This time of year is a very busy time of year for most everyone. In the hustle and bustle of it all, we must remember the reason for the season!

In this sixth week of study, we will take a closer look at the writings of Luke in the second chapter of his gospel account of Jesus' birth. I would like for your minds to wander back in time to try and imagine what it must have been like to be an eye witness to one of the most amazing events in all history.

Anticipate all God wants to teach you this week! Ask Him to show you the things He wants you to see every day as you study His word. Be open to a fresh new approach to life!

DAY 1
O Little Town
of Bethlehem

DAY 2
Don't be
Afraid

DAY 3
Glory to God
in the Highest

DAY 4
Multiple
Witnesses

DAY 5
What Do You
Treasure in
Your Heart?

DAY 1

O LITTLE TOWN OF BETHLEHEM

O Little Town of Bethlehem,
How still we see thee lie!
Above thy deep and dreamless sleep
The silent stars go by.
Yet in thy dark streets shineth
The everlasting Light;
The hopes and fears of all the years
Are met in thee tonight.

If you were to ask me what my favorite Christmas carol is, I would tell you right away that it is *O Little Town of Bethlehem!* When I hear the words to the first verse, I get chills up and down my spine. The reason for the season is summed up in these words...

The hopes and fears of all the years
Are met in thee tonight.

When I look at the Nativity scenes that are so beautifully displayed in homes, yards, and in dramatizations, I suddenly have a peace that takes control of me when I allow myself to stop and reflect on the fact that the hopes and fears of all the years are met in the Christ Child.

In the space below, write a prayer to God thanking Him for sending His only Son to give us hope and to calm our fears.

_____

_____

_____

VERSES FOR THE DAY
At that time the Roman emperor, Augustus, decreed that a census should be taken throughout the Roman Empire. (This was the first census taken when Quirinius was governor of Syria.) All returned to their own ancestral towns to register for this census. And because Joseph was a descendant of King David, he had to go to Bethlehem in Judea, David's ancient home. He traveled there from the village of Nazareth in Galilee. He took with him Mary, his fiancée, who was now obviously pregnant. And while they were there, the time came for her baby to be born. Luke 2:1-6

God's timing is always perfect!

In the space below, write the words from Isaiah 9:6-7.

_____

_____

_____

_____

_____

God is faithful in keeping His word throughout all generations. Isaiah prophesied that a child was to be born who would offer hope and peace. He would rule forever with fairness and justice from the throne of his ancestor David.

In Luke 2:4-7, we find Luke's account of Isaiah's prophecy coming to fruition.

Where was Jesus born? _____

Joseph was a descendant of _____.

Our Messiah and Savior was born in Bethlehem, commonly called "the City of David," due to circumstances beyond Joseph and Mary's control. This serves as a reminder for us that God is in control of our lives too. His timing is perfect, and He has a plan for us just as He did for Mary and Joseph.

As you go through this holiday season, may you be ever mindful of the fact that the hopes and fears of all the years are met through Christ's birth and the fulfillment of prophecy.

His government and its peace will never end.
He will rule with fairness and justice from the throne of his
ancestor David for all eternity.
The passionate commitment of the Lord of Heaven's Armies
will make this happen!
Isaiah 9:7

DAY 2

DON'T BE AFRAID

Have you ever been in deep thought about something or working on a project and had someone suddenly come into the room unexpectedly and startle you? When that happens, what do you do? I usually take a deep gasp and jump. I know others who immediately begin screaming and running away. When I picture the shepherds out in the field tending to their sheep, I often wonder how they reacted when the angel appeared to them.

How do you think they may have reacted?

_____

_____

_____

If you had been in the field that night, how do you think you would have reacted?

_____

_____

VERSES FOR THE DAY

That night there were shepherds staying in the fields nearby, guarding their flocks of sheep. Suddenly, an angel of the Lord appeared among them, and the radiance of the Lord's glory surrounded them. They were terrified, but the angel reassured them. "Don't be afraid!" he said. "I bring you good news that will bring great joy to all people. The Savior—yes, the Messiah, the Lord—has been born today in Bethlehem, the city of David! And you will recognize him by this sign: You will find a baby wrapped snugly in strips of cloth, lying in a manger."
Luke 2:8-12

Luke 2:8-12 is one of my favorite passages in the Bible because it reminds me that God pays attention to each of us at all times and that He chooses different people for different things throughout history. The shepherds just happen to be "the ones" the night of our Savior's birth! Have you ever had someone tell you some exciting news before they shared it with anyone else? I love to be the first to know when someone finds out they are pregnant. I feel privileged to have been chosen to hear this news before anyone else. Just think, the shepherds were chosen to hear the most exciting news of all time before anyone else in the entire world.

This passage also reminds me that the people whom we read about in scriptures are real, just like me. They show fear when something unexpected happens, just like me. They also had to be reminded by the angel not to be afraid because they were going to hear "good news."

In the space below, write down some of the things that you are reminded of when you read this passage.

_____

_____

_____

As you go through this week and think of the events that took place at the time of Jesus' birth, remember to thank God for all He has done for you by sending His one and only Son to earth for your salvation.

Remember that Christ's birth is the reason for the season!

DAY 3

GLORY TO GOD IN THE HIGHEST

Wow, did you read Luke 2:13-14? Can you imagine what that night must have been like? Have you noticed that on really cold and wintry nights the stars seem to shine brighter than they do at other times? What do you think it must have been like to see an angel and a vast host of others in the heavens praising God? It says in the scriptures that "the armies of heaven were praising God."

This was not only a day that the Jews had been longing for, but also the angels in heaven. The time had come for the Savior of the world to be born. It was a time when heaven and earth were rejoicing together because the prophecy of long ago was fulfilled.

Take some time today to reflect on the reason for the season. In the space below, list ways in which you plan to honor Christ's birth this holiday season.

_____

_____

_____

VERSES FOR THE DAY
Suddenly, the angel was joined by a vast host of others—the armies of heaven—praising God and saying, "Glory to God in highest heaven, and peace on earth to those with whom God is pleased."
Luke 2:13-14

Jesus, the Lamb of God
The next day John saw Jesus coming toward him and said, "Look! The Lamb of God who takes away the sin of the world!"
John 1:29

DAY 4
MULTIPLE WITNESSES

VERSES FOR THE DAY

When the angels had returned to heaven, the shepherds said to each other, "Let's go to Bethlehem! Let's see this thing that has happened, which the Lord has told us about." They hurried to the village and found Mary and Joseph. And there was the baby, lying in the manger. After seeing him, the shepherds told everyone what had happened and what the angel had said to them about this child.
Luke 2:15-17

They ran to the village and found Mary and Joseph. And there was the baby lying in the manger. Then the shepherds told everyone what had happened and what the angel had said to them about this child.

If the angel had appeared to only one shepherd, the others might have questioned his testimony. If only one shepherd had decided to go to Bethlehem to check out the validity of the angel's story, the others might have questioned him upon his return with the news. Neither one of these scenarios occurred. There were multiple shepherds in the fields outside the village on the night of the birth. The scriptures are not clear as to how many there were, but it is obvious that there was more than one shepherd that night who witnessed the angel and the vast host in the heavens.

In the space below, write Luke 2:15.

_____

_____

_____

_____

_____

After the angels returned to heaven, the shepherds decided to check this story out for themselves. I don't blame them. I would have done the same thing! Did you notice that they "ran" to the village? When they arrived in Bethlehem they saw first hand yet another miracle...the baby was lying in a manger just as the angel had said. They all witnessed the same thing. It was not just one shepherd but multiple shepherds.

In the space below, write Luke 2:17.

_____

_____

_____

_____

_____

The shepherds told everyone what had happened, and that's how we know about it today!

I am so grateful for the shepherds who were tending to their sheep that night. I am even more grateful that they decided to check the angel's story out for themselves and found it to be true.

What an exciting time of year for us as Christians! We get to celebrate the birth of Christ with our family and friends. Remember the reason for the season, and look up to the heavens today and thank God for the gift of our Savior!

DAY 5

WHAT DO YOU TREASURE IN YOUR HEART?

VERSES FOR THE DAY

All who heard the shepherds' story were astonished, but Mary kept all these things in her heart and thought about them often. The shepherds went back to their flocks, glorifying and praising God for all they had heard and seen. It was just as the angel had told them.

Luke 2:18-20

Having a baby is a very emotional experience for any woman to go through. Mary's pregnancy and birth were different from any other that had come before her or after her. What do you think she may have "treasured" in her heart?

_____

_____

_____

Mary had to be an amazing young woman of faith to have been chosen by God to give birth to His only Son. In the space below, write Luke 1:38.

_____

_____

_____

_____

_____

I believe that throughout the difficulties that Mary faced during this time period, she had a tremendous faith in God and a close relationship that provided her with peace in the midst of her struggles. Mary was chosen by God to fulfill the promise of the virgin birth.

I am grateful for her obedience.

In the space below, write a prayer to God asking Him to show you ways to strengthen your relationship with Him daily.

_____

_____

_____

How is your relationship with God today? Faith in God and a close relationship with Him comes from spending time in prayer and daily Bible study. The more you learn about God, the deeper your faith will become. When you face difficulties in your life, where does your strength come from? I pray that your strength comes from the Lord and that you will treasure the things that He teaches you in His word daily.

As you go through this holiday season, treasure the things that matter most.

The gift of Christ our savior.
The gift of God's Holy Word.
The gift of Hope.
The gift of Peace.
The gift of Love.
The gift of Family and Friends.
The gift of Contentment.

In the space below, list other things that you may treasure in your heart during this holiday season.

_____

_____

_____

HOLIDAY PLANNING
DECEMBER
WEEK 6

SURVIVOR TIPS

When attending a party, there's nothing wrong with buying bakery or deli items.

Take time every day to enjoy some Christmas music.

On Christmas Eve, attend a Christmas Eve church service.

Pick a night during the holidays to go for a drive and enjoy the Christmas lights.

Set out pretty bowls brimming with holiday potpourri; the whole house will smell like Christmas!

Fill a basket with nuts to place on an entryway table.

Candlelight adds so much to Christmas settings. Use them often in December.

TO DO LIST

Christmas Plans:

___ Review calendar, prioritize invitations, programs, and other commitments.

___ Place on-line orders.

___ Cook and freeze appetizers for parties.

___ Finish all wrapping and hide presents or place under the tree.

Christmas is a wonderful time to celebrate family, a warm home, and the joy of the holiday season. Enjoy it with all your heart, and may you have a wonderful holiday season. Tiny Tim said it best, "God bless us, every one!"

DUMP CAKE

1 yellow cake mix

1 can (29 ounces) sliced peaches with juice

½ to 1 stick butter or margarine, thinly sliced

Preheat oven to 350°.

Grease a 9x13 inch pan. Spread half of cake mix evenly in bottom of pan. Pour can of sliced peaches and juice evenly over the cake mix. Cover the peaches with the rest of the cake mix, then slice the margarine on top.

Bake 50 minutes, or until golden brown.

CHERRY-CHOCOLATE CAKE

1 chocolate cake mix

1 cup water

1 egg

1 can (21 ounces) cherry pie filling

Preheat oven to 350°. In a large bowl, mix together cake mix, water, and egg until smooth. Fold in cherry pie filling. Pour into a greased 9x13 inch pan.

Bake 30-35 minutes, or until cake springs back when touched.

PEPPERMINT CAKE

Cake: 1 white cake mix

¾ cup water

2 egg whites

¹/₃ cup vegetable oil

½ cup crushed peppermint candy

Topping: 1 can (16 ounces) vanilla frosting

2½ tablespoons crushed peppermint candy

Preheat oven to 350°.

In a large bowl, combine cake mix, water, egg whites, and oil until smooth. Stir in ½ cup crushed candy. Pour batter into a greased 9x13 inch pan.

Bake 25-35 minutes, or until golden brown. Cool completely.

Spread frosting over cooked cake; sprinkle with crushed candy.

DAILY TO DO LIST:

GIFT-GIVING BUDGET:

Sunday: _____

_____

_____

Monday: _____

_____

_____

Tuesday: _____

_____

_____

Wednesday: _____

_____

_____

Thursday: _____

_____

_____

Friday: _____

_____

_____

_____

Saturday: _____

_____

_____

CHRISTMAS SHOPPING LIST:

_____

_____

_____

_____

_____

_____

_____

_____

_____

_____

_____

_____

_____

_____

_____

_____

_____

_____

_____

_____

_____

_____

_____

_____

_____

_____

_____

_____

GIFTS-GIVEN LIST:

_____

_____

_____

_____

_____

_____

_____

_____

_____

_____

_____

_____

_____

_____

_____

_____

GIFTS RECEIVED:

_____

_____

_____

_____

_____

_____

_____

_____

GROUP SESSION
WEEK 6

THE REASON FOR THE SEASON
Following the arrival activity time, start the group session by reading the introduction page and then open the lesson with prayer.

O LITTLE TOWN OF BETHLEHEM
Have someone read the scripture aloud while playing the Christmas carol in the background. Have members talk about their favorite Christmas carols. Ask someone to read the last three paragraphs on page 114.

DON'T BE AFRAID
Have someone read the scripture aloud. Encourage the members to discuss how they view the events that took place the night the angel appeared to the shepherds. Take time to allow the members to talk about things they are reminded of when reading Luke 2:8-12.

GLORY TO GOD IN THE HIGHEST
Read the scripture on page 117 aloud and ask the members to tell the rest of the group some of the ways in which they plan to honor Christ's birth this holiday season.

MULTIPLE WITNESSES
Have someone read the scripture aloud. Reflect on the events that took place, and take some time for each member to pray silently and thank God for the indescribable gift of Jesus, our Savior! During the time of silent prayer, play instrumental Christmas music in the background.

WHAT DO YOU TREASURE IN YOUR HEART?
Have someone read the scripture aloud. Discuss the things that should matter most during this holiday season as listed on page 121.

Review DECEMBER WEEK 2 of the Holiday Planning guide.

Conclusion.

A Practical Guide to Surviving the Holidays

SOCIAL
GRACES

GROUP SESSION LEADER'S GUIDE

GROUP SESSION LEADER'S GUIDE

Introduction:

SOCIAL GRACES: A Practical Guide to Surviving the Holidays is a six-week Bible study with lessons that provide biblical teachings about how to handle difficult family relationships, holiday spending, social anxiety, and other issues that women may face during the holidays. The lessons will also offer fun and exciting ways to decorate, bake, and entertain in hopes of making this the best holiday season ever.

You do not need a long list of qualifications or years of teaching experience to lead SOCIAL GRACES. You need a heart prepared by God with availability and a willingness to facilitate. As the leader, you will not teach the material; you will simply help others learn for themselves.

Success as a facilitator depends on:

- A heart committed to leading and encouraging others.
- A commitment to complete this study.
- Faithfulness to each weekly meeting.
- A commitment to fulfilling the basic responsibilities described in this Leader's Guide.

Before the Session:

1. Each week complete the daily lessons in the workbook.
2. Pray for each member of your group by name.
3. Pray for God's guidance as you prepare for each week's group session.
4. Arrange your room to meet the needs of your group. An intimate setting seems to work best.

During the Session: Start on time!

At the Introductory Session, inform the members that you plan to start promptly each week. Use incentives to encourage early arrival. How about a chest full of holiday "treasures"? Items such as calendars, highlighters, candles, pens, journals, ornaments, holiday hand towels, cinnamon sticks, wrapping paper, Christmas cards, and baking goods can be used to fill the chest. Tell the members the Treasure Chest will be open 15 minutes before the start time and will remain open until time to begin. If they arrive early or on time, they can get something out of the Treasure Chest. Everyone likes to get a prize. I have used this incentive program and it works! Women who thought they could never arrive anywhere on time are now in the habit of arriving 15 minutes early and feel great about doing so. Great places to shop for Treasure Chest items are at discount stores.

SUGGESTED SCHEDULE

1. Arrival Activity (10 min.)

- If you are serving refreshments, use a different recipe from the Bible study each week. Make sure the food and drinks are ready to be served when the members arrive.

- Share prayer requests – remind the members to be brief and to the point.

- List requests as you receive them so that you can refer to them as you pray.

- Lead the group to pray for each request. Ask God to open the hearts and minds of every member present and for blessings throughout the session.

2. Review the Week's Scriptures and Questions (40 min.)

Start with the introduction page for each week and begin by asking the members to tell you which Bible verses meant the most to them throughout the week. Next, start with Day 1 and ask for brief and basic answers to the questions. This will allow you to confirm that the study content was received and understood.

Questions can be answered by anyone who feels comfortable sharing. Encourage participation. However, do not pressure members to share personal answers, but allow them the opportunity if desired. Ask them to be discreet and not to use names if and when people could be hurt by the discussion. Appropriate discussion of these questions is invaluable to the application of the unit. Be prepared to redirect if at any point the discussion becomes inappropriate. Pray for discretion and boldness to redirect if necessary.

3. Group Session Activities (15 min.)

A wrap-up of the week's lessons should serve as a tool of encouragement as well as a reminder just how much God loves each member individually. Allow time at the end of each lesson for members to swap gift-giving, time saving, and money saving tips with each other. This is also a good time to swap holiday recipes.

4. Conclusion of Session (5 min.)

- Give a brief introduction to next week's study and encourage members to complete their home study.

- Close with prayer. Since prayer requests were taken at the beginning of the session, refrain from asking for them again.

After the Session:

1. While the session is still fresh on your mind, immediately record the concerns of the group members. Remember to pray for these concerns throughout the week.

2. Evaluate the session by asking yourself the following questions.

   - Was I adequately prepared for today's session?

   - Did I begin and end on time? If not, how can I use the time more wisely next session?

   - Does anyone need extra encouragement this week? Remember to follow up with a card or phone call.

Upon Completion of the Six Weeks of Bible Study:

Host a "Drop-In Tea Party" for all of the participants. By using the recipes in this book, you can plan ahead and enjoy spending time visiting with each guest in a relaxed atmosphere. Since the holiday season is so hectic, invite the members to stop by for a cup of tea and some delicious holiday goodies before they attend another social event or in between shopping trips. Be sure and take lots of pictures and have each guest sign their name in your holiday guest book.

For food, gifts, and decorating ideas for the Tea Party, email me at sueann@shineworthy.com.

I thank God for women like you who are committed to teaching, leading, and encouraging others through Bible study. God created each of us for a life anchored in contentment, joy, and rest. Many women feel enormous amounts of stress throughout the holiday season and miss out on what really matters during this time of year. The more they try and get organized, the more disorganized they get. They begin to feel their lives are out of control. Words such as "exhausted," "overwhelmed," and "frazzled" are used to describe their hectic lifestyles.

It is my prayer for you to receive guidance and direction from God as you help others discover ways to survive the holidays. Jesus truly is the reason for the season!

Happy Holidays!
Sue Ann Cordell

Made in the USA
Charleston, SC
16 October 2012